RACE PIMPING

The Multi-Trillion Dollar Business of Liberalism

Kevin Jackson

Published by Wavecrest

Published by Wavecrest
307 Orchard City Drive
Suite 210
Campbell California 95008 United States
info@fastpencil.com
(408) 540-7571
(408) 540-7572 (Fax)
http://wavecrest.fastpencil.com

Printed in the United States of America.

First Edition

Acknowledgments

It's been a while since I have put out a book, as the pressures of writing have given way to a syndicated radio show, and increased speaking schedule, arranging the Reparations Comedy Tour, and trying to build an organization that will change politics forever.

I originally planned this book to be a primer for a lecture series, and not to be taken with a grain of salt. As with all my writing, I bury the lesson in the humor, providing the needed punch in the gut from time to time.

Regardless it takes a team to get all this done. I need to first thank Robert Oliver for providing the blog post that inspired this book. Robert you are a talented person whom the world should get to know.

To my team, I appreciate each of you for tolerating my constant push for perfection. You guys and gals make people think I am a genius and that I'm everywhere, and I simply could not do this without you.

To my extended family, I must always thank you for making me who I am. I wish I were closer, but know that we are working on it! You all inspire me in ways I unfortunately do not get to say often enough.

To my sons, not only do you keep me young, but your amazing intellects and ability to find the laughs are constant reminders of who I am. You will always be my proudest creations.

I owe my inspiration for these books and the time to get them complete, albeit late to Melissa La Boy, my muse and significant other. You are truly beautiful and brilliant, and you possess the cutest shape God could put on a woman. Though your package is spectacular, it is your mind and patience that I appreciate most.

It's all God's plan. I am nothing without my Lord and Savior Jesus Christ. In all that I do, I remember my conversation with God where He said to me, you will never be lost for words or ideas, and understand that I have a plan for you. Thank you Lord for all that you have done in my life.

Contents

Foreword   ix

CHAPTER 1: Black People Need Leaders…who will blame whites!   1

    The Professional Negro   2

    Blame Whites!   4

    Teach love of "blackness."   8

    Equal results, not equal opportunity   9

CHAPTER 2: Defining Blackness   12

    When Whites Were Hot   12

    Defining Blackness   15

    View everything through the Prism of Blackness   20

    Snitches get Stitches   22

    Glorify the Ghetto   24

    Promote Victimology   26

CHAPTER 3: Doing Damage Control   35

    Black Groundbreakers and Trendsetters Don't Exist   35

    Sometimes you have innocent victims.   39

    White Slavery v Black Slavery: Know the Subtleties of Marketing   41

    Say anything, Promise anything but Never Tell the Truth   46

CHAPTER 4: Repeat the Lies   49

    Blacks Don't Research   49

A Short Historical Perspective on Democrats and Republicans   50

Rewrite the Narrative   53

CHAPTER 5: Victory for one black is a victory for all!   57

The Numbers Mean Nothing   61

CHAPTER 6: Black People Can Make It on Their Own   63

ObamaCare: The Cure for all Ills?   66

"Baby Daddy" Syndrome – Thank God for White Feminists   67

The Immigrant Problem   70

CHAPTER 7: Be "Tolerant," but Never Tolerate Diversity   72

A Bit of History on the Thought Police   74

CHAPTER 8: Handling the Media   79

Manipulate the Media   80

It is important that you Establish Your Street "Cred"   81

The Panic Button   86

CHAPTER 9: Going on the Offensive & the Dreaded Black Conservative   90

CHAPTER 10: Promise Everything, Deliver Nothing   95

The Case for Reparations   95

CHAPTER 11: Support Radicals and their Causes   102

Arab racism in the Motherland of Africa is not to be Mentioned   110

CHAPTER 12: Whatever you do, don't educate black people   112

Study Ebonics   115

CHAPTER 13: Monitor Reports of Discrimination Constantly   119

CHAPTER 14: A Sarcastic look at Victimology   126

CHAPTER 15: A Sarcastic Look at Immigration   130

CHAPTER 16: Desperation of race pimp Jesse Jackson   133

CHAPTER 17: Let's apply our techniques to Ferguson, Missouri   135

Justice Arrives   136

Epilogue   141

12 Things The Negro Must Do For Himself by Nannie Helen Burroughs 143

The Poverty Pimp's Poem   147

How to Run an Effective Boycott   148

References   153

Foreword

"That's the way the game goes, gotta keep it strictly pimpin'..."
— Three 6 Mafia

Race pimping knows no color. As for profiteering on race-pimping, black is the old white, half-black is the new black, and white is the old black.

Whether you're black or white, a Liberal, a Democrat, a Progressive, a Liberal Democrat, a Progressive Democrat, or a Progressive Liberal Democrat, you can get a race pass and this book will teach you how to be a race pimp for fun and for profit.

For aspiring race pimps, race-baiters, and other malcontents and meddlers who want to hit the lotto, this is the book for you. If you're going to go through the trouble of creating victims, why not profit from them?

The money in diversity is enormous, even bigger than former sportscaster-turned-political-pundit-turned-sportscaster Keith Olbermann's ego. Liberals claim the money is on the Right, but don't be fooled. If you want to make Kim Kardashian's butt and Kanye West's ego *combined* kind of money, go West, pioneer; as in Left and Liberal.

How many Conservatives do you know who can be crackheads and serve as mayor of a major metropolitan city while dating their chief of staff, AND lie about it? *Save the Kwami for your Mommy, Marion Barry.*

Imagine being a "reverend" who fathers children out of wedlock. I know, bad right? Hold on, Little Johnny, because if you study hard, this book will teach you how to have your non-profit organization pay your mistress *and* your child support – all at the same time.

Have higher aspirations? Why not become a Congressman, where you get the real perks?

By using our proven methods, a Congressman has been able to own New York City slums *and* not pay taxes on his profits. No "Sorry Charlie" for Uncle Rangel.

Think you can get millions for a bank where your spouse sits on the Board of Directors and not go to jail? Not unless you invest in this book, Maxine Waters!

Our proven methods got that Congresswoman a whoppin' $12M, and that's just for starters.

Git some! But you'd better act fast!

Want a cabinet spot with the next president?

HNIC doesn't mean "Hockey Night in Canada!" Check out the Head Negro in Charge of the Department of Justice, Eric Holder, who said:

"...to describe it in those terms [voter intimidation in PA by the New Black Panther Party] I think does a great disservice to people who put their lives on the line for my people."

His people! That's right, Holder has people, and his people are the New Black Panther Party. And Holder's people are the reason Holder used a taxpayer-funded airplane for personal use.

Holder was grilled by Government Accountability Office, specifically Frank Wolf (R-VA) of the House Appropriations subcommittee, and because of good race-pimping training, Holder explained:

"My staff keeps telling me to take it easy, you know, well, this is one that gets me...There was this notion that we've taken — I think it was described as hundreds of personal trips. That was wrong.

GAO counted flights, not round trips. And we looked at it and figured out from the time period that they were looking, we took not hundreds, but 27 personal, four combined — official and non-personal trips — and none of the trips that I took or that the [FBI] director took ever had an impact on the mission capability of those airplanes."

Through our proven methods, Holder turned the tables on them. Holder got indignant, and then said *"Ain't this some shit, it wudn't but 27 times! An' it ain't like we jacked them bitches up all to be damned, Nigga!"*

Soon, you too will feign outrage when you're caught soaking your weenie in the pickle jar. And It just keeps getting better.

Imagine a world where in order to do business with your constituency, Whitey must come through you, and you can get your cut.

Sound too good to be true? Well, it's *not*!

Using the principles of this book can make you a president! And like Barack Obama, with proper motivation you will be using everybody to get what you want, regardless of whether they want it.

Let's all say it together: Unaffordable Healthcare Act!

Consider the opportunities you'll have in academia, for example:

In 2007 the University of Iowa increased its budget for the "administrative costs for affirmative action, diversity and multicultural programs" by 25 percent. "UI expects to spend $738,718 in Fiscal Year 2007 compared to $589,018 in Fiscal Year 2006." [i]

When you consider the number of colleges here in America and multiply that by $500K each – well, you can see the potential. But wait there's more!

Did you catch that budget increase year over year?

In this example alone it's 25 percent — $140,000 more. Why, that's one fast growing pie and it's got a slice with your name on it!

Again…more great news!

When you're race pimping, nobody expects you to accomplish anything. Look at the evidence here:

Non-minority students graduated at a 67 percent rate compared with a 57 percent rate for minority students, according to six-year-graduation rates from 2001 to 2007. [ii]

In other words, success is when you get a D!

And if you think colleges and universities spend a lot on "diversity" with no results, just look at America's corporations.

Companies eat this stuff up, spending *billions* annually on diversity programs. [iii] Soon you will think of diversity as the "soft cost of doing business," a tax on those rich Republican capitalists who are determined to inspire people to better.

One day, you too will make those capitalists pay — well actually the government will do it for you. But you can watch; and that makes it not just profitable, but *fun*!

By investing in this book, you will be taking (or you already have) an important step towards getting your pot of gold at the end of the rainbow. Rainbow. Get it?!

Even metaphors can give you a good hearty laugh, because you can earn big on all "colors" of people, beginning with blacks.

And when you run out of blacks, we'll teach you advanced techniques on how to move to Mexicans, Muslims and even gays.

Become a race pimp with an inflated ego and the bank account to match, all by prostituting the black community (or any community) using white guilt!!

Race pimping is so lucrative, there is a rumor that Chris Matthews will be announcing that he is indeed black. He certainly understands the pimping game. The man is obsessed with "helping" black people. Don't let Matthews get his, before you get yours.

Enough already…Buy this book!

Keep this book to yourself, and do not pass it along for free. We must limit the number of race pimps, because it's a supply and demand game; too many pimps and game off.

Get to work getting yours…while the money lasts.

[1] Ebonics translation: I don't quite understand the reason for concern. We only used the planes 27 times, and we took great care with them, friend.

CHAPTER 1

Black People Need Leaders...who will blame whites!

Black people don't really need leaders any more than white people do. In fact, Liberal black leaders suck!

Ask a Liberal to name a city run by Liberals blacks that is successful, and you might as well as them to divide by pi. Liberals black leaders lead cities into bankruptcy, and not just Detroit.

Atlanta is the city where the mostly white suburbs are splitting off to become their own cities. Why? They are tired of a city that elects only inept black Liberals.

As reported in WND:

These cities, after breaking away politically from urban Atlanta, have become so successful that a libertarian think tank, the Reason Foundation, has featured Sandy Springs as a model of effective government. The Economist has also applauded the northern Atlanta cities for solving the problem of unfunded government pension liability and avoiding the bankruptcy that looms over some urban areas. The new cities may soon be able to create their own school districts, which would free them even further from the issues besetting Atlanta.

While incorporation has been popular with residents of the new cities, not all of Atlanta is as satisfied. The Georgia Legislative Black Caucus filed a lawsuit in 2011 to dissolve the new cities, claiming they were a "super-white majority" and diluting the voting power of minorities. [i]

Whites want to leave the city is so bad, black legislators are passing laws to keep them from leaving the plantation.

Atlanta was supposed to be the NY City of the South, but it's far from it. The crown jewel of black Liberal achievement has been built with fool's gold and cubic zirconium.

What this proves is black Liberals are as lost as last year's Easter eggs. They have been decimated by Liberal policies dating back decades.

Don't you fret! There is still plenty of opportunity for you to get in on the race-pimping, though you will need to act fast.

Your new job is to fool black people into thinking they need leadership. They must look to a black Moses to lead them into the Promised Land, and Moses is your middle name.

To quote the Bible-toting Aunt Esther of *Sanford and Son* fame, "Hey glory!"

The Professional Negro

Black people must believe in you, so the first order of business is to make you "Professional Negro." [1]

Black writer and radio show host Armstrong Williams' comments about the character of the "Professional Negro," or one who wants to make a good profit from his blackness:

"The black pseudo leader is a parasite. He nourishes himself on the suffering of others. He exists by satisfying the mob's voracious appetite for excuses and easy solutions. If there is no easy solution for the complex problems of racism in our country, the black pseudo leader will create one. In a calm baritone he will talk about reparations. Sure, that causes people in the crowd to pump their fists in support...[O]ur leaders spend all their time cleaving to century-old crimes and stirring racial tensions because this is how they make a living." ii

The professional Negro is explained further by black radio talk-show host and author Ken Hamblin. To be successful at pimping your sole purpose in life, is *"hustling, intimidating, manipulating, using any means possible to achieve (your) goal in getting something for nothing from Whitey's system."*iii

The professional Negro is an historical figure, recognized by former slave and educator Booker T. Washington, who wrote in 1911:

"There is another class of coloured people who make a business of keeping the troubles, the wrongs, and the hardships of the Negro race before the public. Having learned that they are able to make a living out of their troubles, they have grown into the settled habit of advertising their wrongs — partly because they want sympathy and partly because it pays. Some of these people do not want the Negro to lose his grievances, because they do not want to lose their jobs... I am afraid that there is a certain class of race-problem solvers who don't want the patient to get well, because as long as the disease holds out they have not only an easy means of making a living, but

also an easy medium through which to make themselves prominent before the public." iv

You'll soon join this new class Williams, Hamblin, and Washington describe, and become a professional race pimp in no time by using our accelerated method.

So what the days of the struggle for Civil Rights at the hands of racist Democrats are over. No sense telling anybody, now is it. *There's gold in "Dem" hills!*

During the heyday of the civil rights movement, our community leaders were not apt to become household names unless they accomplished something great, something galvanizing. Things have gotten much easier.

Today's leaders can achieve this lofty perch by pumping people full of vitriol about how all the problems we face as communities are the result of other people's sins. They fill their speeches with the sort of racial rhetoric that shocks people into paying attention.

If you can manage to do this, your followers will confuse the attention you receive with genuine black leadership.

As long as black Americans are in the dark, and Americans in general are "Snooki stupid," opportunity awaits you.

Let's get one thing clear. If you're not willing to extort people and compromise your ethics, then stop right here, as race-pimping is not for you.

Blame Whites!

Professional Negroes always blame whites. It's been like this for decades, so why change a winning formula?

Author and TV commentator Tony Brown writes: *"America's black leadership sees its primary function as blaming whites for the dire problems of the black community and demanding more government intervention as the sole solution to this predicament."*[v]

So what if blaming whites is nonsense? That's not the point.

These teachings force black folks to be angry at white folks for no other reason except that white people for the most part are easily recognizable. Remember, they are "not black."

Constantly remind your black constituency that white folks owe us, regardless if the facts are accurate or not. Black "reparations movement" leader Dr. Conrad Worrill accomplishes provides an example here: [vi]

"The Trans Atlantic Slave Trade and Slavery, Expropriation of Our Labor, Slave Codes Laws, Destruction of the African Family, Raping of African Women, Fugitive Slave Laws, Colonizing of Our African Culture, KKK Night Riders and Lynchings, The 13th and 14th Constitutional Amendments (purported to be a "scam,"), Denied Our 40 Acres and a Mule, Jim Crow Laws, Fighting and Dying In Imperialist and White Supremacist Wars, Assassination of Black Leaders (Malcolm X, Dr. King, Fred Hampton, and Mark Clark), COINTELPRO, Crack Epidemic, Criminalizing Our Youth, Jailing of Freedom Fighters, Centuries of Mis-Education and Mental Atrocities "which has caused serious damage to our people, and continues to cause much mental confusion about our true reality as an African people in America and around the world."

Forget that much of this damage was caused by black Africans, white Democrats, and black Americans. Using evil, rich, white Republicans as the reason for the destruction is the easier sell.

White people owe us; especially Conservative Republican white folks. We will get the government to take what's ours from them.

The key is to look for the nearest white man to blame. Think, *"Reginald Denny!"*

Do you remember what Reginald Denny did to black people?

Reginald Denny had the nerve to be doing his job and driving through a black neighborhood when the Rodney King verdict was read. He also had the bad sense to be born white, too.

No beating of a white man was more deserved than the beating Reginald Denny got, now was it?

If you can learn to think like this, your investment in this book will pay off in spades (pardon the pun), because you'll be successful at this endeavor and free at last to peddle your black community to the Democratic Party.

Let's look at Eric Holder. This is a man who should be in jail.

Eric Holder hates white man's law. He feels that laws proposed by white men are unjust, thus his animus towards America.

Yet, in his departure from the Department of Injustice, the Left will depict the most racist and incompetent Attorney General in America's history as Moses the Lawgiver; a man who was for the common man. The Attorney General for civil rights.

Is this process great or what!

We are a country where radical black Nationalists like Eric Holder have taken control and do as they wish, and they use the media as puppets in their political theater.

In 1968 there was a confrontation by Holder, et al with police as reported here:

"Armed with guns, the students took over Hamilton Hall, and locked the building from the inside. After some time the black students told the white sympathizers, many of whom were members of Students for a Democratic

Society, to leave and contribute by taking over other buildings on campus. They did, effectively shutting down the university. The president of the university ordered the NYPD to smother the protest by force, aided by white athletes and members of the ROTC. Ironically it was the white students in other buildings who bore the brunt of the police storming. Had the police broken into Hamilton, they may have suffered casualties at the hands of the sisters and brothers inside."

Two years later, Holder was among the leaders of the SAAS that were demanding the former ROTC office be renamed the "Malcolm X Lounge" in honor of the early Black Muslim leader who was assassinated in 1965. [vii]

What is Holder's legacy?

Holder got crack cocaine similar sentencing as regular cocaine, so now crackheads and cokeheads have the same standing. I don't know about other black people, but this potential-crackhead-turned-black-Conservative is excited!

I can hardly wait to keep not doing drugs.

We know that Holder is notorious for protecting the rights of black teens. Whether it's college-bound Trayvon Martin or gentle giant Michael Brown, Jr. Holder is on the case to remind people that justice is black. Holder doesn't need evidence, just tell him who's black and who's white or white Hispanic, and it's on like a chicken bone.

What Holder won't do is explain to America why the Obama administration is running assault weapons into Mexico, or why the government spies on its own citizens.

Holder won't explain why under his watch, the Justice Department cracked down on journalists reporting on national security matters, secretly subpoenaing Associated Press phone records and used a search warrant to obtain some emails of a Fox News journalist as part of a separate leak investigation.

In an interview, Holder expressed that his biggest regret was "the failure to pass any responsible and reasonable gun safety legislation after the shootings in Newtown." Holder got a conscience on guns with this school shooting, but not all the shootings that happen in black neighborhoods all over America every day.

Now I ask you how a Black Nationalist radical like Holder could be put in charge of the Department of Justice unless he had a hookup? You're reading how, Silly!

Teach love of "blackness."

You will learn how to teach your black constituents to love their blackness more than they love Jesus and more than they love common sense. Remember, it's all about the blackness.

Regardless of who is in the White House, make sure you're not in the outhouse. – Kevin Jackson

So what if America has a black president; that doesn't mean anything has changed.

Though millions of white people voted for a black president, there were many racist whites who didn't.

See how easy that was!

Don't allow what one group of white people did supersede what the bad white people didn't. Understanding this will improve profits on your people, n-fold.

N-fold...now *that's* funny!

You come with a price; and it's a high price. When people call you to demagogue an issue, you get an honorarium; no exceptions.

If a black church wants you to discuss a shooting of a black child by a cop, they must pay $20,000 for you to show up. If the cop is white, then the price goes up to at least $50,000.

When it comes to hot racial incidents wherever they may be, you answer the Blackphone, head down to the Blackcave, fire up the Blackmobile, and drive to the nearest TV camera and microphone to blame [*insert white Conservative Republican most applicable at the time*], to get lots of media time and to build your prominence. The more prominence, the more Benjamins — and it's all about the Benjamins.

***

Equal results, not equal opportunity

Don't just demand equal opportunity, demand equal *results*!

If every black family is not movin' on up and living in Beverly Hills, then America is racist, and rich white people are stepping on the necks of blacks. It's the government's responsible to fix this inequity. We want justice and we want it now. *No justice, no peace!*[2] Keep demanding the government do what it's not designed to do.

Demand the government ends poverty now. Tonight!

So what it if will never happen; that's not your issue. So what if we fought the war on poverty and poverty won. The battle must go on.

The good thing about fighting poverty is it's a fight we *can't* win. So we get to keep fighting the war.

We know the poor will not be self-sufficient, and the objective is not to suddenly make them self-sufficient; like they could handle it. Psst.

The poor just need to *think* we're fighting for them; for "hope and change." We make them think we'll build a society where everybody is equal, where the janitor has the same social status as the CEO, and eventually will earn the same. Fat chance!

The real objective is to accomplish nothing (see Chapter 10), as empowering the poor would be disastrous.

If the masses of people found a way to get out of poverty, why would anybody need you? Your funding sources would dry up. You'd be in the unfortunate position of having to find a real job. That would SUCK! Just ask any hardworking, taxpaying Conservative!

You're in this game for three reasons — reputation, power, and money, and don't you forget it.

Tolerance is a word you'll need to learn, and we will cover it in more depth in Chapter 7.

***

You should always be ready to protest and be ready to lead a few choruses of "*We Shall Overcome.*" Protests allow black people to hearken back emotionally and subconsciously to the days of civil rights marches and to create more white guilt. Marches galvanize the black community, as blacks have been conditioned for decades to see marches as somebody fighting for their rights. It is important you tie into that emotional chord, as itwill help you sell victimization.

Dr. Martin Luther King, Jr. proffered the ridiculous concept of judging a person by the content of his character and not by the color of his skin. *Nonsense!*

As a professional race hustler, you must first, last, and always judge a man by the color of his skin and not by his character.

Welcome to the Black Taliban. Who knows? You may be the next African-American Idol [viii]!

[1] Do this quickly, because soon the government may require a license, with fee!

[2] Favorite quote of Sharpton while marching against "white oppression."

CHAPTER 2

Defining Blackness

"Few people are more contemptible than some self-anointed Keeper of Negritude who attempts to teach other blacks how to be black."
— Black columnist Bill Maxwell

When Whites Were Hot

There was a time in American history when being white was "the bomb."

For much of American history, racist Democrats had white people convinced that they were the superior race, so much so that people like Margaret Sanger only wanted enough black people around to serve white people. History is replete with white Democrats and socialists from peons to heads of state who believed the lie of white superiority.

Imagine being conditioned to believe that you are best, only to find out that you are quite mediocre. That the best people had been hidden from you—to protect your fragile ego.

In the early days of entertainment, America had "white music" — people like Pat Boone, the Rat Pack, and Andy Cuomo. It took black men like Little Richard and Chuck Berry to put some peanut butter on that white bread. Music would never be the same.

We had TV shows like The Dick Van Dyke Show, My Three Sons, and Hazel. White, white, white.

Those show, or shows like them, dominated TV. Then came Sanford and Son, The Jeffersons, and Good Times to the TV entertainment world, and with those shows another cultural earthquake. Television would never be the same.

From the booty call, the electric boogaloo, the cabbage patch, the centipede, the cha-cha slide, chicken noodle soup, the dougie, the cupid shuffle, da butt, the bump, the electric slide, the humpty, krunking, the moonwalk, the prep, pop locking, the robot, the roger rabbit, the running man, the snake, the stanky leg, to the tootsie roll…there's nary a white dance among them.

Black people invent a new dance every other year, it seems. White people haven't invented a dance in a hundred years (except the "White Boy", of course).

Watch old films of "white basketball," and you wouldn't recognize the sport of today.

Remember when white guys shot free throws underhand? The NBA would have been NFL (Not For Long) if it weren't for Julius "Dr J" Erving, George "The IceMan" Gerving, and other innovative black ballers.

Magic Johnson gave the sport the "no look" pass and somebody black invented the finger roll, while Kareem Abdul Jabbar gave us the "sky hook." Whether it's the "alley oop," or the "cross-over dribble," it was black players who innovated basketball.

In baseball, the Negro league consistently beat white professional teams, on the rare occasions when white guys were willing to be embarrassed. Inte-

gration of "white" baseball may have been a step up financially and culturally for black players back in the day, but that transition was undoubtedly a
step down in competition for black players.

Jackie Robinson revolutionized baseball in many ways, yet he was considered a mediocre player in the Negro League. Josh Gibson, not Babe Ruth,
was the real home run king, hitting over 800 home runs and against black
pitchers. Gibson hit 69 home runs in only 134 games, with no juicing!

Satchel Paige made Cy Young look like a slacker. It is said that Paige
pitched 29 games in one month, and won 104 of 105 games at one point in
his career.

Remember the white NFL, when guys took their helmets off, folded them
up and put them in their pockets? No? Me either.

Ernie Banks and Jim Brown and the like are the reason the NFL had to get
new helmets. And Gayle Sayers faked many a white defender out of his
shoes.

I have one name for you in track and field: Jesse Owens. 'Nuf said, Adolf. [i]

In boxing, remember when white guys "put up their dukes?" You've seen
those pictures of the guy with one fist way in front of the other. What was a
clumsy club sport was changed to an art by people like Jack Johnson, Joe
Louis, Muhammed Ali, and Sugar Ray Robinson, to name a small few.

Whites have slipped dramatically in stature over the past decades, eradi-
cating any idea that they are the "superior race," as if one there is such a
thing. Black people have proven time and again what they bring to
America.

And who knows where blacks would have been had it not been for the
destructive meddling of Democrats.

This is the reason you have this tremendous opportunity!

With the rich history of achievement by blacks in America, you'd think that blacks today would not lament American history, but instead celebrate it. This goes to show you how easily you will be able to manipulate them.

Black Liberals don't need to know that no ground has been lost for whites by blacks stellar record of achievement and creativity, and that black creativity is American creativity. Just keep reminding black people that they need you.

Defining Blackness

If you're white and reading this, don't be dismayed. Black does not necessarily mean "color." It's much more than that. Blogger LaShawn Barber sums it up well:

"The very word 'black' is not only a skin color or race; it's code for a set of prescribed behaviors and attitudes. Being authentically black means meeting a set of criteria, including thinking like other blacks (read liberal), displaying certain 'black' behavior, exacerbating racial tension, and voting for Democrats." [ii]

You must be so black that if you eat sushi, watch reruns of *Dawson's Creek* and *Friends,* or enjoy the ballet, you will hang yourself. If you don't fit this meme, you may qualify as being "authentically black."

You must be so black that simply owning a white dog could get you labeled an "Uncle Tom."

"Blackness is existential Play-Doh: It's biology, it's ideology, it's sociology. Blacks are liberals and Democrats. Blacks support affirmative action and marry other blacks. Blacks never criticize other blacks 'in front' of whites. Bill

Clinton was the first 'black' president because he had no daddy, poor nutritional habits, played the sax, and was sexually self-destructive." [iii]

Using these narrow-minded standards, native Africans, West Indians, Haitians, and so on do not count as "black." You must count them as "foreigners," nothing more.

"As a black immigrant and a Haitian-American who has lived in the country for 37 years, I know how it feels to have my blackness challenged by native-born blacks... Many of my black immigrant friends have also had their blackness questioned by native-born blacks who see us as 'not really black.' My ancestors probably weren't enslaved on American soil, but they were enslaved on Haitian soil. So how am I less black or less worthy of kinship with black Americans? How ridiculous that someone would think me unable to understand the pain of racism and the long-term costs of white supremacy and slavery." [iv]

Even Kwame Raoul, a Haitian-American who filled Barack Obama's former seat in the Illinois State Senate, said he too has encountered skepticism from black voters for his ethnic background and for his name. [v]

Willis Shalita, born in Uganda and a naturalized U.S. citizen, felt the sting as well:

"I, too, have been told that I am not a true black American. But who sets the bar? Who defines what it means to be a black American?

"Surely connections to slavery should not define our identity and our destiny. Africa, too was colonized, but Africans have moved on. They don't con-

tinue to try to make hay from that chapter of their history. African Americans should take heed." [vi]

Orlando Patterson, a black West Indian educator explains it this way.

In recent years, however, this tradition has been eroded by a thickened form of black identity that, sadly, mirrors some of the worst aspects of American white identity and racism. A streak of nativism rears its ugly head. **To be black American, in this view, one's ancestors must have been not simply slaves but American slaves.** *(emphasis added) Furthermore, directly mirroring the traditional definition of whiteness as not being black is the growing tendency to define blackness in negative terms—it is to be not white in upbringing, kinship or manner, to be too not at ease in the intimate ways of white Americans."* [vii]

According to this measurement the late Jamaican black leader the Honorable Marcus Garvey, former South African president and anti-apartheid leader Nelson Mandela and Archbishop Desmond Tutu of South Africa are not really black or are not black enough.

In order to avoid the pitfalls of non-black blacks who have come before you, it is necessary for me to introduce the Black Authentication System: [viii]

THE BLACK AUTHENTICATION POINT SYSTEM: START WITH 0 POINTS

SPEAKS PROPER ENGLISH – MINUS 15 POINTS

SINGLE PARENT HOUSEHOLD – ADD 2500 POINTS

GREW UP EATING MIRACLE WHIP SANDWICHES – ADD 5 POINTS

GOT BAD GRADES – ADD 20 POINTS

GOT GOOD GRADES – MINUS 55 POINTS

WENT TO PUBLIC SCHOOL – ADD 15 POINTS

WENT TOPRIVATE SCHOOL - MINUS 20 POINTS

HAVE KIDS BEFORE 18 – ADD 10 POINTS

GOT MARRIED BEFORE YOU HAD KIDS – MINUS 15 POINTS

OWN A BIGGIE OR TUPAC CD – ADD 25 POINTS

CAN PLAY BASKETBALL/FOOTBALL/TRACK – ADD 20 POINTS

CAN'T PLAY SPORTS – MINUS 75 POINTS

CAN DANCE – ADD 30 POINTS

CAN'T DANCE – MINUS 300 POINTS

EATS FRIED CHICKEN, MAC AND CHEESE, COLLARD GREENS ANDCORNBREAD – ADD 20 POINTS

EATSSTOVE TOPSTUFFING – MINUS 60 POINTS

OWNS A PAIR OF TIMBS OR JORDANS – ADD 35 POINTS

HAS A FRIEND IN JAIL – ADD 30 POINTS

DOESN'T KNOW ANY CRIMINALS – MINUS 25 POINTS

HAS ACREDIT SCOREOVER 700 – MINUS 25 POINTS

HAS ACREDIT SCOREUNDER 600 – ADD 25 POINTS

HAS A CORPORATE JOB THAT REQUIRESBUSINESSDRESS – MINUS 5 POINTS

HASA JOB – MINUS 1 POINT

ON WELFARE – ADD 10 POINTS

ON FOODSTAMPS – ADD 10 POINTS

CONSTANTLY CHEATS ON HIS GIRL – ADD 40 POINTS

WANTS TO BE FAITHFUL AND MARRY HIS GIRL – MINUS 70 POINTS

REFERS TO AND TREATS WOMEN LIKE B#TCHES AND HOES – ADD 750 POINTS

TREATS WOMEN LIKE QUEENS – MINUS 1375 POINTS

GETTING AMASTERS DEGREE – MINUS 20 POINTS

DOESN'T HAVE A GED – ADD 20 POINTS

KNOWS HOW TO FIGHT – ADD 30 POINTS

WOULD DUCK AND/OR RUN – MINUS 35 POINTS

HATES THE POLICE – ADD 40 POINTS

SALUTES THE POLICE – MINUS 150 POINTS

YOU HAVE A MIXTAPE AND REALLY THINK YOU'RE GOING TO BE A RAPPER - ADD 200 POINTS

YOU DON'T EVEN LIKE RAP MUSIC – MINUS 400 POINTS

***

View everything through the Prism of Blackness

Everything your constituency does or think must be viewed through the very narrow prism of blackness. They must talk black, walk black, think black, read black, eat black, drink black, dress black, smell black, sneeze black, cough black, yawn black, surf the Internet black, and even urinate black. Failure to do so has consequences. Take soccer for example:

"Soccer is considered a 'white' sport. Now when I say 'white' I'm not talking about the snow, you sillies. I'm talking about it being a sport that is mostly played by little white boys and girls in America. I realized very quickly that little black girls stuck out like a sore thumb on a soccer field. I remember the other activities that children my age (and color) were getting into around that time. Basketball, baseball/softball, and football were the most popular sports being played, and I would always inquire why no one wanted to play soccer. These are the replies I received from my peers, 'Soccer is for white people! It's boring and stupid!' That confused me greatly. I knew that I wasn't white, and that soccer was far from boring and stupid! But I left it alone and simply enjoyed my first few years of soccer with my head held high, and a bajillion trophies." ix

It is totally irrelevant that many black Africans, all over the continent play soccer. However, we have already proven that black Africans are not authentically black anyway.

However it's not just sports, as black columnist Bill Maxwell explains:

"For committing an act of pure decency, three black women are being ostracized by many other black people. On the night of June 29, Delores Keen, Renee Roundtree and Rose Dodson rushed outside Keen's apartment after

they heard gunshots. They discovered two Tampa police officers, David Curtis and Jeffrey Kocab, lying together on the ground. The officers had been shot. Dontae Morris, a 24-year-old black ex-convict, would be charged in the shootings.

"Roundtree checked the officers' pulses, and Keen dialed 911. The three women stayed with the dying officers until others arrived. The Hillsborough County Commission honored the women for trying to help the officers.

"Since their identities were made public, the woman have been criticized by fellow blacks almost everywhere they go, walking down the street, at local social clubs and in stores.

"Their sin, considered by many to be perhaps the worst in American black culture, was helping 'the enemy' — the police. You are guilty of helping the enemy in two main ways: You give the police, or another authority, information about a black person who has committed or is suspected of having committed a crime, which is 'snitching.' Or, as is the case with the three women, you physically aid and comfort police in distress, which is treated the same as snitching.

"By trying to help the officers, Keen, Roundtree and Dodson showed, in the eyes of many, that they are not 'Authentically Black.' They are traitors to their race.

"'I even had an ex-friend call and say, "That was f——- up. You turned my boy in," ' Roundtree told the St. Petersburg Times of a response to her attempt to help the officers.

"The snitching ethos, or code of silence, runs so deep that many blacks who snitch or assist morally struggle with their decisions. Many apologize, while others, having acted, offer history and background as to why blacks see the police as the enemy.

"One of the ugliest public displays of the snitching ethos occurred last year when Anderson Cooper interviewed rapper Cam'ron for 60 Minutes. Cooper asked Cam'ron what he would do if he knew he was living next door to a *serial killer. Cam'ron said he would move away rather than snitch on the killer."* [x]

Snitches get Stitches

It should be clear now that the police are the enemy of black people, NOT simply the black criminal element, especially our beloved drug lords and gang member thugs in our communities. You must impress upon your constituency that to be authentically black (and to live to see tomorrow):

"Thou must not snitch to the cops or thou wilt suffer the consequences." – written on the Tomb of the Unknown Former Black Snitch

"A black mother of five testified against a Northeast Baltimore drug dealer. The next day her row house was fire-bombed. She managed to put out the flames that time. Two weeks later, at 2:00 a.m. as the family slept, the house was set on fire again. This time the drug dealer broke open the front door and took care in splashing gasoline on the lone staircase that provided exit for people asleep in the second- and third-floor bedrooms. Angela Dawson, the thirty-six-year-old mother, and her five children, aged nine to fourteen, burned to death. Her husband, Carnell, forty-three, jumped from a second-story window. He had burns over most of his body and died a few days later. On that chilling night, as she struggled against the smoke and heat, the mother's cries could be heard over the crackle of the flames on East Preston Street. 'God, please help me,' screamed Angela Dawson. 'Help me get my children out.'

"Before she was silenced, Dawson made thirty-six calls to the police, from late July until her death, to complain about the drug dealers who operated freely on the street in front of her house.

About a month before she was killed, one of the dealers had scrawled BITCH on the front wall of her house. As she was scrubbing away the graffiti, a young man who lived across the street, an eighteen-year-old, appeared and boldly said he had written the word there, told her to leave it alone, and then hit her.

"The teenager who slugged her, John L. Henry, was charged with assault. He was already on probation for carrying a gun. But after a brief court hearing, he was sent home, and the very next day two bottles of burning gasoline came crashing through the Dawson's kitchen window. Then, two weeks later, the blaze was set that burned down the house and killed the family. The man charged with setting the fatal blaze lived next door to Henry.

"The murderer was Darrell Brooks, twenty-one, a convicted car thief known in the neighborhood for criminal activity with the '281 Crew.' The gang spray-painted vacant buildings where they did drug business with the letters RIP. Police later described Brooks as a small-time drug trafficker who sold heroin and crack. As part of a plea deal to avoid the death penalty, he confessed to having set that earlier fire that burned the Dawson house. According to police records, Brooks had told other young men in the drug trade in East Baltimore before the first fire that he planned to burn the family out because 'Mrs. Dawson is snitching on people.' Brooks pleaded guilty to the crime of killing the five children and two adults in exchange for a sentence of life in jail without parole." [xi]

Lesson: If you're thinking, "Don't blame Darrell Brooks for what he did," then you are on your way to profitability.

This poor misguided black man was not responsible for what he did. The legacy of racism and slavery made him slaughter that black family. In other words, the white man made him do it!

***

Glorify the Ghetto

An essential element of authentic blackness is to "glorify the ghetto." Blogger Danielle Belton weighs on this element in "Definition of Blackness:"

"Black poverty romanticized to the point where the actual pain of the inner city is a soundtrack to the affluent, white and black. A mother mourns her teenage son, a scholar, whose [sic] life is cut short by a stray bullet. It is recycled and remixed to bang, bang, bang, drop the rocks, it's hot on the block, f*ck 'em, I don't care, I got cheddar in hand, I'm the pimp of a mother's prayer....It's emphasized in our music, in our literature, in our art. County Brownies would try to prove who was the most 'down' by dropping gratuitous 'nigga this' and 'nigga that.' They bragged about going to 'the city,' to hang out with the real 'niggas.' They knew folks. They Crip Walked. They kicked it with the hardcore. Because the city was where the real blackness was. The badassery for douchebaggery. The city was where you could be down.

"But a County Brownie could switch in a minute. They didn't like the deseg kids. They were bused in because of some court ruling. Something about integration. But no one cared. The deseg kids were anathema. They were lower than low. Their clothes weren't cool and they didn't talk right. They didn't act right. I'd call it classism, but that was a dirty word in blackland. In the authentic black identity there's only one class and it has no class.

"I was raised in an all black suburb called Hathaway Manor North. It was the kind where all the white people fled when my parents and other blacks moved in. All the people were married. All the kids were relatively good. The neighborhood was relatively crime-free and peaceful. Everyone had good jobs —teachers, principals, ministers, letter carriers, postal workers, union day laborers, business owners, middle managers, white collar execs. It was what you'd hope a black community would be. Everyone looked out for one another. Everyone knew each other. Everyone pitched in to make it a nice place to live.

"I loved my old neighborhood, but when we moved to the 'white' part of the county when I was 13 things changed. I remember how excited the few black kids at my new junior high were because I was from 'tha hood.' I was from the ghetto. I was supposed to be realer than real, shittier than shit because Hathaway Manor was O-Dog tough, or so they heard.

"They wanted to know about the gangsta shit. They wanted New Jack Suburbs. I didn't understand. How could a Hathaway be 'tha hood' with manicured lawns and teachers/preachers' kids? But they told me I was wrong. That I didn't know my old neighborhood and school. They told me dystopian fantasmas of Nino Brown and fights everyday, of the cops being there every day. Of crack-fueled sexcapades and things of Donald Goines [http:// en.wikipedia.org/wiki/Donald_Goines] novels.

"That I was a black girl lost to a dopefiend's whores waiting on Kenyatta's last hit.

"But I was dullsville. I wasn't cool. I had no stories of break-ins and drive-bys. I'd never been in a fight. I didn't curse and I spoke perfect English. I didn't use any slang harder than 'Gee whiz,' 'dang' and 'gosh.' I liked classical piano and drawing cartoons on my notebooks. I liked history and English and Tevin Campbell songs. I dreamed of holding his hand while he sang "Can We Talk." I dressed like "Blossom."... I can sing almost every Negro spiritual. I have southern roots that I love. I have two black parents and I was raised in a black neighborhood. I went to an all black elementary school. I know my black history up and down. I know my African roots.

"My skin is brown. How could I not be black? What on earth is blackness? What are the rules?

Should I perm my hair bone straight? Should I wear it in an afro? Should I drop some 'niggas' in my speech? Should I love Jay-Z and listen to Lil Wayne? Should I grow dreads? Should I get into Pan African culture and start wearing dashikis? Should I live on the hardest block in St. Louis' North City? Should I smoke Phillies? Should I engage in Jesus flavored braggadocio? Should I be real cool and leave school? Lurk late and strike straight? Sing sin and thin gin? Jazz June and die soon?

"Who is black?... But when I find myself preferring Dave Grohland Rilo Kiley, preferring 'white' rock music and Lena Horne jazz standards am I betraying blackness? When I won't watch a Tyler Perry film but will run to a Martin Scorsese production, is that a sin? When I find that I can relate more to my white co-workers who have done more and seen more than the put-it-all-on-the-Lord-in-Prada churchniks *I met. The ones who didn't watch films with subtitles or listen to music without words. Did I betray blackness then?*

"I was forever in a Negro wasteland of stunted vision." [xii]

In other words: If it ain't ghetto, it ain't black.

***

Promote Victimology

"To be authentically black and faithful to their race, blacks must not achieve on their own. They must view themselves as eternal victims and reserve at least a minimal resentment against white America." — Lloyd Marcus [xiii]

University of California at Berkley Associate Professor John McWhorter schools us on what we promote best — "Victimology":

"What, then is the essence of 'black'? One sometime answer is 'Being down with us,' and that down is telling. A large part of being culturally black means operating under a fundamental assumption that all blacks are a per-

secuted race, still 'down' at the bottom of [the] well, forty years after the Civil Rights Act....Victimology, like any virus, infects in degrees—it bypasses a few, leaves some bedridden, but leaves most with at least a persistent cough.....Only when (the)victimhood one rails against is all but a phantom does one have the luxury of sitting back and enjoying the sweet balm of moral absolution undisturbed. [xiv]

Professional race baiters must give kudos to black woman victimologists like Mary Anigbo, Principal of the Marcus Garvey School. She told *Washington Times* reporter Susan Ferrecchio, who was reporting on the school's progress in 1996 where to get off.

Before Ferrecchio left the school, she was asked to show her notes, which is against journalistic protocol. Ferrecho refused.

Principal Anigbo told Ferrecho: "Get your white ass out of this school!" Then she had some of her students take the notebook and physically assault her. University of California at Berkley Professor John McWhorter writes of the incident:

"Anigbo first accused Ferrecchio of pulling a knife on a student, then denied the episode ever happened, then claimed that Ferrecchio had deserved it." [xv]

Such black women do us a service by instilling in their black students the conception that Whitey is the eternal enemy; that Whitey is picking on black schools, and that uncivil behavior by blacks is accepted in an academic setting.

But wait! There's more. An Associated Press article reported:

"In a trial laced with racial overtones, the principal of a District of Columbia charter school was found guilty Friday of assaulting a newspaper reporter who visited the school for a story.

"Superior Court Judge Truman Morrison found Marcus Garvey Public Charter School Principal Mary Anigbo guilty of assaulting Washington Times *reporter Susan Ferrechio on Dec. 3(1997).*

"Anigbo also was convicted of assaulting two police officers and of taking the reporter's notebook.

"Three other school employees were convicted of related charges. All of the charges were misdemeanors.

"Anigbo denounced the convictions as racist and likened herself to martyrs throughout history.

"'I'm in very good company. Who can I name who was lied upon, who was pushed and shoved?'

Anigbo said outside the courthouse. 'I can name Jesus Christ, Martin Luther King, Marcus Garvey and Sojourner Truth. I can go on and on.'

"Anigbo and one of the school staffers face up to 15 months in jail and fines of up to $2,300. The other two face up to 180 days in jail and $1,000 fines. Anigbo will be sentenced Oct. 15.

"Anigbo's attorney, Veronice Holt, vowed to appeal the verdict. She also said Anigbo would sue the newspaper and the Police Department. The newspaper did not immediately comment." [xvi]

Sister Anigbo showed you exactly what to do when you are caught assaulting people and get arrested.

You claim to be a martyr, a victim, and liken yourself to Martin Luther King, Jr. or even Jesus Christ. You cannot go any higher than that. Claim that Whitey knows you are dangerous and that's why he wants you in jail. Many blacks, and even some white liberals will believe you.

For good measure, have some picket signs pre-made with "FREE BROTHER [insert your name]!" or "FREE SISTER [insert your name]!"

Think "Trayvon Martin" and the hoodie, or the most recent race baiting opportunity with Michael Brown's shooting by a cop in Ferguson, Missouri.

Make some "WHITEY OWES US!" signs too and have your people ready to use them as soon as you get arrested. Think of the valuable publicity you will get.

"It is almost analgesic to talk about what the white man is doing."[xvii] - Bill Cosby

You must make talking about the white man as addictive as crack, and as natural as breathing.

Author and radio talk-show host Ken Hamblin provides evidence of the success of our strategy in his book *Pick a Better Country*.

The following is a radio conversation in 1996 between Hamblin and a proud black victim caller (thoroughly under our control) named "Bruce" from Memphis:

Bruce: *"I'm telling you right now that as a black man, I will die before I allow you to take my affirmative action, my food stamps, my welfare. Now, I have the ability to unite with other black men, I have the intelligence to equip devices..."*

Hamblin: *"Stop a minute, stop a minute....Your passion is imprinted on me, and if you go much further you're going to get yourself into trouble, and I don't want you to do that....You're threatening mayhem....Let me tell you something. I'm a fifty-five-year-old colored guy, brother Bruce, and the last time I heard that kind of fervor and commitment from people of color in this country was when black Americans were sitting at a lunch counter in Greensboro, North Carolina, demanding full access and entr ée to the American system, which we now have. And now you're looking for a guarantee. You're looking for the government to support you through welfare and affirmative action and quotas, and that's insulting and demeaning to the history and the legacy and the spirit of those great Americans who said, 'Give me a chance to participate.' A chance to participate is not a guarantee."*

Bruce: *"I'm a ninety's nigger and I'm not going to take anything from anybody. You're going to give me my affirmative action and my programs or... I'm just going to say or else...I'll be a guerilla warrior. I'll come to you. I'll bring you pain. I'll bring a riot and you know what's goin' happen? You gonna give it to me. I don't know why we got to play these little games."*

Bruce is proof that our program of victimology is a success!

Hamblin: *"But today there are people like Bruce to harbor a fanatic commitment to the ghetto, to their 'community.' Instead of being confined there, they control and stake claim to this territory, because it represents dollars from the government. They know that, for the most part, Whitey will pay to ease his guilt and his fear through taxpayer-supported government programs designed to appease these 'nineties niggers.'*

"The politicians I call poverty pimps are the brokers, the middlemen between the government and the people in Dark Town.

"I call them poverty pimps for good reason. The white elected officials who are their counterparts must produce pork barrel offerings in the way of industry and jobs to further the economic well-being of their districts in order to retain the support of their voters.

"But these politicians have convinced their constituents, most of whom are black trash, to settle for the dead-end political spoils of government welfare.

They devote their entire political careers to procuring more welfare and poverty-program dollars for their stagnant districts, and thus I call them poverty pimps. " xviii

Hey, Hamblin described us to a "T"! You are now Authentically Black.

***

Now that we have established what is "Authentically Black," hating white folks should be fun for you.

You must be a black Svengali, hypnotizing your black constituency into believing their victimhood must be thoroughly embraced and enjoyed; or they might do something dangerous to you like getting educated, thinking independently, and leaving the plantation.

You have to get black folks happy and grinning when they get out of bed, saying to themselves, "Man, I wonder how the white man is going to try oppress me today…whatever!"

In "The Ironic Joys of Underdoggism" in Associate Professor John McWhorter's book *Losing the Race* he pens:

"[M]any black people decrying their supposed victimhood so do with joy rather than the despair one would expect. The Reverend Al Sharpton is a useful illustration. Here is an excerpt from The New York Times shortly after the murder of Amadou Diallo:

"'Just before the evening news the other night, the parents of Amadou Diallo, the West African street vendor shot dead by plainclothes police officers last week, walked up to a microphone to offer their first extended public remarks

about the death of their son. The setting was a second-floor auditorium up a scuffed flight of steps in Harlem. And the host, wearing a crisp, gray three-piece suit and clearly enjoying this latest bustle at his Harlem headquarters, was the Rev. Al Sharpton.'

"But wait a minute. A man has just been killed and his bereaved parents just stepped up to the microphones. Why is Sharpton enjoying himself? The reporter was not a racist subtly slurring Sharpton—all of us are familiar with the air of exuberance about Sharpton each time something like this happens. The reason is that he delights in this kind of thing. Wouldn't a genuine response to victimhood be indignation? Wouldn't we expect especially a reverend to be consumed with remorse about such a tragic death? But no—Sharpton, as always, reveled in the cheap thrills of getting to stick it to Whitey one more time by cloaking blacks as eternal victims and whites as the eternal oppressor…Yet this pathologically misplaced joy goes far beyond politicians, percolating deep into the black community. I recall a decidedly Afrocentric schoolteacher describing to a group her life thus far as a litany of discrimination and marginalization because of her color. I cannot speak for the validity of her interpretations of all these events. What I could not help noting, however, was that all of this was delivered with a beatific smile. One would naturally expect someone who had truly suffered to register pain and resentment—refugees from the Soviet Union and battered wives do not tell their stories with a grin. One does not delight in the noose around one's neck or the fire on one's skin. The only possible explanation for someone deriving pleasure from victimhood, besides outright sadomasochism, is if the victimhood addresses a lack inside of them…What this woman reminded me of was not a Holocaust survivor but our classroom tattle-tale, who betrays that his motivation is less uplift than personal absolution by the glee with which he reports the torts of others…The Cult of Victimology has forced people like this schoolteacher into wearing victimhood like a badge and reveling in it for the joys of underdoggism that it brings. There is a certain seductive charisma in this—this woman could definitely hold a crowd—but it has nothing to do with moving the race forward."[xix]

As a black Civil Rights professional, you are not interested in moving the race forward. You are the doctor who is not interested in curing the patient, because a sick patient keeps paying and paying.

Your goal is to get your people to waste lots of time talking and hearing about how the white man is oppressing them, and that for black people, there is no such thing as "The American Dream."

Except when there is.

Writer and noted black Conservative Shelby Steele tells the story of a black friend:

"I have a friend who did poorly in the insurance business for years. 'People won't buy insurance from a black man,' he always said. Two years ago another black man and a black woman joined his office. Almost immediately both did twice the business my friend was doing, with the same largely white client base." [xx]

The explanation of this anomaly is simple. The other black man and woman were just not black enough and those white folks just felt sorry for them. That is why they gave those blacks their business and made money. Steele explains it:

"Integration shock is essentially the shock of being suddenly accountable on strictly personal terms. It occurs in situations that disallow race as an excuse for personal shortcomings and it therefore exposes vulnerabilities that previously were hidden. One response to such shock is to face up to the self-confrontation it brings and then to act on the basis of what we learn about ourselves. After some struggle, my friend was able to do this. He completely revised his sales technique, asked himself some hard questions about his motivation, and resolved to work harder." [xxi]

Clearly the brother lost touch with his victimhood. Unfortunately, he may be successful in his business and will no longer be able to blame white folks for his poverty.

What a tragedy!

Your constituents must believe that whites continually burn the midnight oil thinking of new, innovative and creative ways to oppress black people.

The Almighty White Man on High will always do his best to hinder black progress, and it can even be guised as something that actually does help black people. Your people will know "them honkies have the power to keep us black folks back into slavery" in perpetuity, and any help they give is just based on their guilt, and it's never enough. Your people must wallow in powerlessness and have the almighty white man on their minds constantly, a technique discovered on the old plantations in the ante-bellum South.

Keep hate hope alive!

CHAPTER 3

Doing Damage Control

"Y'all gon make me lose my mind, up in here, up in here. Y'all gon make me do some time, up in here, up in here. Y'all gon make me ack a fool, up in here, up in here. Y'all gon make me lose my cool, up in here, up in here."
— DMX

Black Groundbreakers and Trendsetters Don't Exist

When blacks find out that other blacks are breaking barriers, you absolutely have no choice but to step in. You need to do some damage control.

Ursula Burns, a black woman, became CEO of Xerox. Your response? That never happened, and it is an ugly rumor. Tell them she does not exist; she is an urban legend. No black could EVER become CEO of Xerox in the "system" of white man's Amerikkka.

Kenneth I. Chenault, a Black CEO of American Express? Not remotely possible.

***

Pop Quiz: Is Kenneth Chenault authentically black? [1] (see answer below)

***

A quick review of victimology reminds us that your minions must have an 1850's mindset that blacks cannot get anywhere in this country. If blacks start giving you tangible examples of black progress, learn from this black man speaking with Tony Brown:

"A black man told me that my socioeconomic status could only be explained because I was 'chosen' for success by white people. The stereotype that he has internalized of himself makes him believe that external circumstances (white people) determine his worth. Conversely, failure for most blacks is the result of not being chosen by whites. And, of course, whites will only allow a handful of blacks to do well, the self-confirmed victim argued." [i]

We expand upon victomology, as we make our people believe that white people choose black people for success or failure. The point: black ignorance can work for you equally as well as white guilt.

Keep the legacy of slavery, Jim Crow, Black Codes, KKK, lynching, segregation, poll taxes, and so on, in their faces. Teach your followers to say things like "You owe us!" and "We are never gonna get over it, Whitey!"

Never let Whitey forget it, as you must bring these white folks down to their knees!

How do you shake the money tree of white guilt?

"Jesse Jacksonis the master of the corporate shakedown. His tactics are tried and true. Jackson first fires off a letter to a corporation criticizing it for not hiring enough minorities. He demands a meeting. If the corporation defends itself and rejects the demands, Jackson publicly accuses said organization of racial insensitivity, announces a protest and calls for a boycott. Since corporations recoil at charges of racism, they usually attempt to appease Jackson and agree to a meeting. The upshot is that Jackson can claim a historic breakthrough that also produces a corporate contribution to Jackson's Rainbow Push Coalition." [ii]

Washington-based watchdog organization Judicial Watch reports:

"As early as 1982 Jackson launched a boycott of Anheuser-Busch because it purportedly did not have enough black-owned distributorships nationwide. The beer company eventually contributed $510,000 to Jackson and established a $10 million fund to help blacks buy distributorships. When Jackson's two sons (Yusef and Jonathan) purchased a River North distributorship in Chicago for an estimated $30 million, Jackson dropped the boycott and became the company's best friend.

"Jackson has gone so far as to lobby the Federal Communications Commission to block companies seeking government approval to merge, until they donate money to his organization. In the late 1990s, he opposed the merger of telecommunications giants SBC and Ameritech, saying it would be detrimental to low-income customers.

"Money changed Jackson's mind, however. He became the deal's biggest cheerleader when the companies donated $500,000 to one of his Rainbow/ PUSH funds.

"Shortly after that, he opposed a merger of AT&T and TCI but, once again, reversed his position after AT&T wrote a $425,000 check. Fearing the wrath of Jackson's racism accusations, other telecommunications giants – including GTE and Bell-Atlantic – followed suit with big contributions." [iii]

And let not forget another master of the shakedown, Al Sharpton:

"Anheuser-Busch gave him six figures, Colgate-Palmolive shelled out $50,000 and Macy's and Pfizer have contributed thousands to the Rev. Al Sharpton's charity.

"Almost 50 companies - including PepsiCo, General Motors, Wal-Mart, FedEx, Continental Airlines, Johnson & Johnson and Chase - and some labor unions sponsored Sharpton's National Action Network annual conference in April.

"Terrified of negative publicity, fearful of a consumer boycott or eager to make nice with the civil-rights activist, CEOs write checks, critics say, to NAN and Sharpton - who brandishes the buying power of African-American consumers. In some cases, they hire him as a consultant." [iv]

In discussing one professor of pimpology Al Sharpton, writer Akindele Akinyemi wrote:

"I feel it's a damn shame that Black liberals are always protesting and demanding White people be fired for saying something stupid yet we give

Blacks who consistently call or sisters bitches and hoes on a regular basis a free pass. We degrade our race by trying to live like Good Times or live out our lives in poverty. We enjoy sagging our pants in public, even in church where it is supposed to be a House of God...We call Black women freaks, hizzoes, hoes (yes even nappy head hoes), tramps, pigeons, dykes, jiggas and skanks. We call each other niggers (oh I forgot we graduated, now we call each other niggas), fags, and other dreadful names. We never demand Wendy Williams from being fired or other Black personalities who call other races disrespectful names. I have heard Black personalities and Black liberal leadership call Whites 'crackers' and 'redneck hillbillies' but if a White person call us 'hoes' we demand the removal of that person from the station."
v

Promote the doctrine that whites are devils, capable of mass genocide; except by abortion [2]. Remember, genocide is very close around the corner.
vi

***

Sometimes you have innocent victims.

There are times when you can do nothing. The damage control is simply ignoring the incident.

A case in point happened in December 1996, when Charles Davis, a black police officer, was murdered by robbers while trying to protect Ira Epstein, owner of a check-cashing store where Davis was moonlighting.

Author Jim Sleeper chronicles:

"[S]pectacles of slain officers, grieving families, and ranks of police in parade dress seldom fire the liberal civic imagination. (Certainly there was no outcry from liberal activists or institutions over Davis's murder.) Liberals who can recite with near reverence a roll call of black victims of white hatred —Rodney King, Yusuf Hawkins (a black youth set upon and murdered by a gang of whites as he walked innocently through their Brooklyn neighborhood), Michael Griffith (chased by young whites to his death on a parkway in Queens's Howard Beach), Darrell Cabey (paralyzed for life by subway gunman Bernhard Goetzin 1984), and many others—would be hard put to recall whites murdered by blacks, especially if the victims are police officers.

"But liberals forgot Charles Davisfor a different, more troubling reason: He, like his killers, was black. That barred him from the pantheon of martyrs that would have received him had his killers been white. In a cruel irony, some of the black victims who did gain admission to that pantheon had records of criminal violence, like the men who killed Charles Davis...Just as murders register more strongly in the traditional racist imagination when committed by blacks against whites, they register more strongly in today's liberal imagination when committed by whites against blacks. Both mindsets, blinded by color, eclipse the human reality that transcends it. In reality, most murders involve perpetrators and victims of the same race. In reality, proportionately more such murders are black-on-black than white-on-white. In reality, according to the Federal Bureau of Criminal Justice Services, more blacks in the United States are killed by other blacks in a single day than are killed by whites in a week. (At this rate, the Ku Klux Klan will have to go out of business because of nothing to do—Authors) Yet black victim after black victim is lowered into urban America's choking soil without a word from any liberal commentator, activist, or politician, black or white.

"Charles Daviswas one of those victims. Once upon a time, he would have been a liberal hero in death, because he would already have been a liberal hero in life. He wasn't New York City's first heroic black cop, but his winning personality and his effectiveness with fellow officers and the public transcended race in ways liberals used to admire. Surely he did more to break down racism in the NYPD than any critic of police racism has done. Yet, now, he seemed as invisible to most liberals as he would have been vivid to their predecessors. When he was killed, there were no memorials to Davis or *expressions of outrage toward the suspects by liberal advocacy groups whose members had taken to the streets over white-on-black murders. There were no protests by Al Sharpton, New York's premier impresario of racial street theater."* [vii]

A casualty of war. Get a '40 and pour a drink for our homey. No whitey, no helpy.

***

White Slavery v Black Slavery: Know the Subtleties of Marketing

If anybody counters white slavery in America with black slavery in Africa [3] or the massacre of 800,000 blacks by blacks in Rwanda, ignore them. *Damage control.*

The story of Boko Haram has all the makings of a Hollywood movie featuring Barack Obama with Jackson and Sharpton advising in the Situation Room.

223 Nigerian school girls have been abducted by terrorists and threatened with slavery. The authentically black avengers spring into action.

On advice of Sharpton and Jackson, Obama orders the Osama-like hit, and a team of Black Ops specialists take over. Obama orders the drones be released.

"African-Americans" get their Hollywood ending as the Black Ops team finds the terrorists and takes them out, rescuing the 223 young Nigerian girls from a life of male-dominated oppression.

But you have heard nothing about this real-life terrorist drama from Obama, and other race-baiters here: [viii]

Pressure was growing on Monday night for Western military drones to be used in the hunt for more than 200 schoolgirls abducted in Nigeria, as the terrorist thought to be holding them threatened to "marry off" girls aged as young as nine.

The urgency of the situation was underlined yesterday when Boko Haram, the Islamic extremist group believed to have abducted the girls, released a video in which its leader gloatingly threatened to sell them as "slaves".

Even with Michelle Obama holding up her sign—showing all that support—nothing has happened.

Apparently, like black on black crime, "black on black" slavery doesn't count for America's race-baiters. "African Americans" don't seem to give a rat's butt about the potential for slavery with 223 young Nigerian girls, and here's why.

First, America's silly Liberal Negroes could not care less about The Motherland.

What happen in Africa, stays in Africa!

Second, there is no money in this type of slavery. There is no white man to threaten or intimidate, only other Africans. And like the first slave trade of Africans selling other Africans, there can be no mention of that by "African Americans."

Let this be a lesson to you. You are not interested in black-on-black genocide at all. Only white-on-black genocide is a tragedy worthy of recognition. Blacks killing other blacks is never as bad as whites killing blacks.

You need to spotlight high profile cases of white racism and genocide that will boost your reputation, power, and money. If anyone tries to make any useless cases of black genocide, such as Rwanda, Sudan, or the aforementioned Nigerian kidnapping public, consider them hecklers, and be prepared to shut them down.

It's as true today as it was in the past.

Former Black Nationalist Gerald Ball learned that true black leadership ignores black-on-black oppression:

"I am a black man, a former nationalist. I became disillusioned with 'black unity and nationalism' during the massacre in Rwanda and Zaire during the mid-1990s. It seemed to me, a student at a historically black college at the time, that black progressives did not lift a finger to protest or press our government or the UN to act to prevent the slaughter amongst black Africans the same way they did apartheid, Haiti, or even the plight of the Palestinians. Why not? **Well for one, because there was no white victimizer oppressing people of color, both parties were of the same race.** *(emphasis added) But the main reason was that our black American leadership did not want our intervention in Africa to cost Bill Clintonand the Democratic Party politically. Getting Bill Clintonand some other white Democrat governors, congressmen, and senators re - elected to preserve our puny little integrationist affirmative action and welfare programs was worth more to us than the lives of hundreds of thousands, possibly millions, of our African brothers and sisters.*"[ix]

Ball is not alone in his analysis, as Conservative black blogger La Shawn Barber discusses the abandonment of South Africa:

"It is neither profitable nor psychically satisfying to speak out against or address black-on-black violence. So-called black leaders and others inclined to protest have no interest in chastising their own people for living careless, reckless, fruitless, and crime-saturated lives. Guilt-tripping whites are where the money and other perks are." [x]

Years ago when apartheid in South Africa was in style, we marched, protested, yelled, screamed, got arrested at South African consulates, etc. We were all determined that black South Africans would not be under the rule of a white minority government, right? Now there is no more apartheid. We left the black South Africans to fend for themselves. Now South Africa has one of the highest crime rates in the world. [xi]

If there are no white faces are involved, ergo no white victimizers, there can be no victims.

We were all vocal against apartheid, but were we vocal against the slaughter of black Africans in Darfur, Sudan? Of course not. Move along. Nothing to see here. Why? See previous paragraph.

Instead, you must give out an endless supply of "black passes."

"In the past, black Americans have given sparse attention to the wretched excesses of Mobutu and other black African leaders, compared with the relentless pounding we have given, albeit with good reason, to white South African leaders." [xii]

A brother wrote on his website *The Field Negro*:

"These atrocities against our people take place in other parts of the world, while African Americans choose to do nothing. *We go to Durham North Carolina and speak out against the Duke lacrosse team for allegedly raping one of our sisters, or to Mexico to confront their President for making derogatory remarks about us, but there is silence while thousands of black Africans are being slaughtered on a daily basis...I have seen more white people involved in this struggle, and trying to bring this issue to the forefront than blacks. And for that, we as black folks should all be ashamed. The UN called this the worst humanitarian crisis in the world, and still black folks in this country remain silent. No outcry, no marches in Washington organized by black leaders, no ink from the black press, nothing; just silence."*[xiii]

Silly Field Negro, Trix are for kids!

Someone should let this brotha know there's no fun (or money) in protesting other black folks.

Samuel Cotton, a black American journalist who visited North Africa and was an eyewitness to the slave trade going on there now wrote about *Black Africans who journeyed from all over the United States in 1995 to meet at Columbia University. Mauritanians and Senegalese from Washington—Ugandans and Sudanese from as far away as Ohio, would spend two days discussing the beast that continues to bite deep into African flesh—slavery.*

This slave trade is common knowledge in Congressional circles and shamefully, Black leaders have not educated the African-American public on an issue central to their history." [xiv]

Lesson: Ignore black-on-black oppression here and abroad. You cannot generate any white guilt (or dollars) from black-on-black oppression, so don't waste your time.

***

Damage control will be necessary.

It's easier when you keep your black folks scared and angry, as you encourage them to satisfy their thirst for "freedom" [4] by drinking from the cup of bitterness and hatred.

Who cares about the high plane of dignity and discipline? Never let them know there is such a thing as "personal responsibility." That's a white man's concept [5], and we want nothing to do with anything white.

You are your constituents only friend and voice. Romance them. Wine and dine them, so to speak. Appeal to their egos. Make them feel superior by way of making them feel inferior.

Make them feel that the "outside communities" of all ethnic groups will never accept them. You must actually control and isolate your people, rather than really care about them. Do everything to make them feel good, to make them want to be "movin' on up" just like *The Jeffersons*. Promise them a "piece of the pie," but don't you dare give away any pie.

Say anything, Promise anything but Never Tell the Truth

As Jack Nicholson said to Tom Cruise in *A Few Good Men*, "You can't handle the truth!" Your constituency cannot handle the truth. The truth is they must stay on the mental and social plantation that has been created for them by the white liberal Democrat establishment, as that keeps them dependent on you. You want to be popular enough so that your word is law. You want them to trust your judgment without question.

Why will they believe you? Because you are *authentically black*!

"Black Americans have been encouraged to accept without equivocation the veracity and nobility of all black 'leaders.' This was not always the case; in the early days of modern civil-rights activism (that being the late nineteenth and early twentieth centuries), blacks claiming to speak for black advancement had their work cut out for them as far as gaining the trust of their would-be constituents went. Now, the latter-day compulsory allowance on the mere basis of being black has been the case for so long that critical evaluation of said leaders is no longer even considered. Whether they be activists or politicians, as long as they spout black power, entitlement, and victimization rhetoric, they are acknowledged as legitimate representatives of the black community."[xv] He also writes: "Blacks will unequivocally trust a black activist or politician who tickles their ears, despite the fact that most of the mundane miseries they encounter are perpetrated upon them by other blacks...Since they are black, they're unassailable even if they are blatantly hypocritical, so atremble are many whites over being branded as racists."[xvi]

"Most ordinary Black people rarely question the legitimacy of their Black leaders and their White liberal manipulators. Many Blacks hold to the myth that Whites, and particularly White Republicans, are the primary obstacles to Black empowerment. And so the Black elite maintains its position and control over the masses by failing them and blaming the failure on Whites, and specifically on Republicans, some of whom deserve the condemnation. But even if the White conservatives fell in love with Blacks and the White liberals stopped exploiting them, would anything change? No, because the Black liberal elite and its wealthy rip-off artists would still be there to bleed the trusting Black masses." [xvii]

This is key; so pay attention:

Black elected officials are never to be held accountable, whether they are caught kiting checks, taking kickbacks, running slum tenements, or buying crack cocaine. Black elected officials committing crimes are a badge of honor in the black community. We must always come to their defense and blame the white man for their actions. We could not care less if our leaders are redeemable or not.

A black Democrat Liberal Progressive congressman from Louisiana stashing ninety-thousand dollars in his freezer can easily be explained. His actions were a result of the legacy of slavery and the idea that the white man caused us to steal and hoard our food.

It's not criminal. It's *ancestral*!

Also, always preach that affirmative action is our birthright!

We black people have the right to settle for crumbs and to believe we will always be dependent on someone else, especially the federal government.

[1] Answer: How black can he be? He has a French name.

[2] Never ever attack the rich white abortion industry!

[3] Which has been going on for 800 years

[4] Freedom they already have!

[5] Acting White!

CHAPTER 4

Repeat the Lies

"If you repeat a lie often enough, it becomes the truth."
— Attributed to Joseph Goebbels, Reich Minister of Propaganda in Nazi Germany

Blacks Don't Research

In humor there is truth, and there is a saying, *"if you want to hide something from a black man, put it in a book."* [1]

Do you think your constituency will actually question you or do any research to find out if what you are saying is true or not? Black Liberals believe that study and research is for white folks.

So always, always, always, (and don't get that out of order) accuse the Republican Party of being the organization whose main goal in life is **and always has been** black oppression.

You must repeat this lie over and over again to your people, because repeating the lie reinforces it. Over time, the lie will not be questioned.

Provide visualization. Say things like *"All whites have white sheets and hoods in their closets."* [i]

A Short Historical Perspective on Democrats and Republicans

Never talk about the fact that the Republican Party was started to limit the expansion of slavery in the mid 1800's and to abolish it. Never talk about the fact that only Democrats, and not one Republican, were the slave masters and that the Democratic Party supported slavery in the past.

Never ever talk about how the original white Republicans were anti-slavery and after the Civil War, helped former slaves to have political power before the Jim Crow days. If someone writes a book or lectures on those historical facts, claim that all was a myth; that it never happened. Say the white Republicans are trying to bamboozle black folks. [2]

Claim that no Republican EVER voted for any Civil Rights Act. As I said earlier, your followers won't bother to challenge that blatant lie. That's what makes this so fun. Most will think like former black Democratic activist M.D. Currington from Sacramento, California, who thought the worst Democrat was better than the best Republican. [3]

Never talk about how all the first black representatives in state and federal government were 100% Republican. Claim that all was a myth as well because it was really the Democrats who freed the slaves, under their most famous Democratic president Abraham Lincoln.

Never reveal the hidden secret that Democratic Party hero President Woodrow Wilson, a Southerner, segregated the Federal Government in Washington, D.C. soon after he was inaugurated. Booker T. Washington said of his visit to Washington, D.C. in the summer of 1913: *"I have never seen the colored people so discouraged and bitter as they are at the present time.*[ii]

In *Wrong on Race* Bruce Bartlett writes:

"African Americans were also dismayed by Wilson's policy of replacing black political appointees with whites in positions they had held for many years through Republican and Democratic administrations.

For example, the American envoys to Liberia and Haiti, as well as the Register of the Treasury, had traditionally been blacks. Wilson replaced them all with whites, denying blacks even the tiniest bit of political patronage...By 1916, most blacks who had voted for Wilson in 1912 realized they had made a terrible mistake" [iii]

Never ever talk about how the Republican Party was the party blacks overwhelmingly supported until the late 1930's. Claim this fact as a myth and the Democrats always had the backs of blacks.

Act as if black Republicans such as Senator Edward Brooke and civil rights activist James H. Meredith never existed. Claim that Martin Luther King always voted Democrat, which was not true.

Never talk about the majority Republican support for the 1964 Civil Rights Act. Always say it was a Democratic victory and not a Republican one.

Make up the story that says Republicans in Congress resisted, even filibustered, the Civil Rights Act. Make your people remember the Republican Party is the Party of the Devil. Make your people believe that the Democratic Party has always championed civil rights, despite the fact it really has not and goes through pains to hide its racist history from blacks. [iv]

Black Republicans are wicked devils.

Hint that any black who votes Republican could be concerned about their physical health and should have good hospital insurance and even better life insurance.

"Any African-American who votes Republican is a turncoat." — Jesse Jackson

Misinformation is good.

If you must, say it's illegal for blacks to vote Republican. If you get blacks to believe Abraham Lincoln was a Democrat and all the slave owners in the ante-bellum South were Republicans, riches await you:

*"While interviewing people on the streets of L.A. and N.Y. for our documentary about the legacy of the Civil War, we came to the staggering realization of how many allegedly well-educated people assumed that **Abraham Lincolnwas a Democrat fighting slave-owning Republicans in the South**,"* (emphasis added) writes Yervand Kochar.* [v]

They will want to believe your every word and be your greatest cheerleaders. And if you are challenged on your scholarship, cry "Racism!" and say "How do I know that whites folk's history is accurate?" Say that white folks have been writing their version of history for thousands of years. If you must lie, make your lies very good, very elusive, and *very profitable.*

If someone claims the number one problem in the black community is teen pregnancies and the percentage of black children born out of wedlock jumped from 25% to 70% in the last 30 years, change the subject, ignore him, or find some reason to blame slavery and the white man for that. Moral issues in the black community are not your concern.

Always talk about the majority black prison population. Even though there are some wrongful convictions, tell all the inmates, even the ones who are actually guilty, that it is no fault of theirs they are in prison. Also tell them that white society is unfair to punish them because their actions are due to this repressive white system and slavery. The white man made them they way they are and they are not responsible for their choices. Always blame Republican administrations, especially Ronald Reagan. That will go over very well with your people.

If you are caught in a crime, blame poverty, family abuse and, above all, racism for your predicament. [4] After all, it is not your fault. You are a victim.

The legacy of slavery, racism, and the Almighty White Man emasculated you, and you had to lash out and do something anti-social. You had no choice in the matter.

When you become a prominent professional in the civil-rights industry, always claim the white man is trying to bring you down, even if that is not true. Remember, black people never do or say anything wrong, even when they do. White people always do or say everything wrong. Whether they do or do not is irrelevant.

***

Rewrite the Narrative

Another tactic you need to promote yourself is, if you do not like current black history, just write your own. Make up a believable story with a "color" of scholarship. Give your constituency a "myth to live by."

Stanford University black educator and author Thomas Sowell writes:

"The form in which the story of slavery has reached most people today has been along the lines of the best-selling book and widely-watched television mini-series, Roots *by Alex Haley. Challenged on the historical accuracy of* Roots, *Haley said: 'I tried to give my people a myth to live by.'"*[vi]

If the white man lied to black folks all these years, then honest black folks can lie to black folks too.

"Haley embarrassed his true believers by taking folklore and fictional liberties with a narrative he'd claimed was historically true. He fabricated 'discoveries' about [Kunta] Kinte and even recycled others' fiction , settling out of court for $650,000 with author Harold Courlander, passages of whose novel The Africans *he had pretty much copied. C. Eric Lincoln recalls that many members of the Black Academy of Arts and Letters considered* Roots *fraudulent in literary as well as historical terms because they viewed Haley as less than a true writer and the book itself as more cinematic than 'interior' in the ways that written fiction can be."*[vii]

Writer John White recounts:

"Like every black person I know, I got caught up in the Roots *frenzy. So I was shaken when one of my professors of African history told me that Haley's soul-stirring account of tracing his ancestorKunta Kinte [http:// en.wikipedia.org/wiki/Kunta_kinte]back to his Gambian home village of Juffure was a fairy tale....Over the years, the strict factuality of* Roots *has been challenged persuasively in all sorts of ways, and I am not trying to reopen that controversy. Most people I've talked to seem to agree with [Dr. Henry Louis]* Gates, *who thinks the book should be regarded as a brilliant 'work of the imagination.' Even Haley conceded that* Roots *was a blend of fiction and fact that he labeled a 'faction.'*[viii]

Lesson: Learn to be *"factional."*

Audrey Peterson further illustrates this point in the *American Legacy* website of black urban legends you are expected to promote:

"One is that a black man named John Hanson was the first president of the United States. I wrote about this tale in an editor's letter in the Fall 2001 issue of American Legacy, *but because I've had more queries about it lately, I thought I'd address it again here.*

The story goes that on November 5, 1781, a John Hanson of African descent was elected the first president of the Continental Congress under the Articles of Confederation, the precursor to our present Constitution. This is a type of historical urban legend that has been circulating for years and is incorrect. The John Hanson who became the first president of the Continental Congress was a white man of European descent. The black John Hanson was a senator of Liberia in the mid-nineteenth century." [ix]

John Hanson is a black protagonist that brought "Fake Change we could have believed in!"

***

"The barriers to black progress in America today are clearly as much psychological as they are social or economic. We have suffered as much as any group in human history, and if this suffering has ennobled us, it has also wounded us and pushed us into defensive strategies that are often self-defeating. But we haven't fully admitted this to ourselves. The psychological

realm is murky, frightening, and just plain embarrassing. And a risk is involved in exploring it: the risk of discovering the ways in which we contribute to, if not create the reality in which we live. Denial, avoidance, and repression intervene to save us from this risk. But, of course, they only energize what is repressed with more and more negative power, so that we are victimized as much by our own buried fears as by racism." [x]

Let's just put some clothes on this naked truth, because there is a lot more to be gained in doing so.

Look at a shining example like Senator Elizabeth "Fauxchahontas" Warren. She went from fake Indian to real Senator, and now she's being discussed as a potential presidential candidate!

And you thought you couldn't win the lotto.

[1] Or on a scholarly website.

[2] Rev. Wayne Currington lectured on the true history of the Democrats. Some blacks stood up and accused him of lying.

[3] He later learned the truth, and was none too happy about it.

[4] A thief gave the excuse, "It's Reagan's fault. Reagan made me take it!" for stealing a cheeseburger from a hospital cafeteria.

CHAPTER 5

Victory for one black is a victory for all!

"If Barack Obama wins, we win!"
— Attributed to a former Connecticut black activist

Singer songwriter Al Jareau could not have said it better: "We're in this love together…it's like the kind that lasts forever."

So when one black wins, we all win right?

It was certainly like that in the early days. When boxer Joe Louis beat that white German Max Schmeling years ago, the nation won. Black people depended on that win. What would have happened had Louis lost?

Poet and author Maya Angelou, among others, recounted her recollection of the Louis-Schmeling fight while growing up in rural Arkansas, listening to the fight over the radio in her uncle's country store. While Louis was on the ropes, 'My race groaned. It was our people falling. It was another lynching, yet another black man hanging on a tree…. this might be the end of the world. If Joe lost we were back in slavery and beyond help. It would all be true, the accusations that we were lower types of human beings. Only a little higher than the apes ....'

"Conversely, when Louis won the fight, emotions were unbounded:'Champion of the world. A Black boy. Some Black mother's son. He was the strongest man in the world. People drank Coca-Cola like ambrosia and ate candy bars like Christmas.'" [i]

Years later, that scenario played out in a very different way.

Protagonist Muhammed Ali would be pitted against antagonist George Foreman.

Foreman had been declared the "sellout," because he was being supported by white devils who wanted to shut up newly Nation-of-Islam Muslim-ed Ali.

Foreman even had the nerve to hold up an American flag in an interview.

When the fight was to take place, Foreman brought his German shepherd to Zaire, which black people took as Foreman's reminder to blacks of white oppressors using these dogs to intimidate black demonstrators.

Fun Fact: "Foreman was called an Uncle Tom by many Afro-Americans when he held an American flag in his hand as he stood on the victor's stand at the 1968 Olympics." [ii]

Ali went on to defeat Foreman, vindicating black people that Foreman was indeed a white devil in black skin. With the Ali win, black people had dodged yet another racist bullet.

Fast forward to 2008.

Blackness was again facing the firing squad. Would America go black in our biggest fight in history? America went black, and elected a man who though only half black would be accepted as a bona fide black president, and not an honorary one like Bill Clinton.

The election of Obama made blacks feel good about "history," but it did not necessarily change their own personal situation or their communities.

"As I reflect on the first two years of Obama's administration, I am becoming more convinced that many of us in the Black community have been guilty of living vicariously through the achievements of Obama to the extent that we have superimposed his individual victory on our race as a whole. Though he is making progress on many of his promises, we are not benefiting in the way we thought." [iii]

Obama's election made many blacks feel like, "We run things now!"

A black woman quit paying her rent after Obama was elected president. She said "We have a new president and things are going to change."

A young black man stole a bag of chips from a store on the night of November 4, 2008, election night. He felt since we had a black president, he did not have to pay.

A relative of comedian Kevin Craft said after Obama's election: *"F**k white people! Black folks ain't gotta do sh*t."* [iv]

Translated: Black people won't have to do anything to get ahead, because we are large and in charge.

A woman in Texas thought that Obama was going to make black people all "rich." [v]

Everybody knows that woman in Florida is still waiting for a check from the White House so her mortgage gets paid. [vi] If you happen to find her, you can bet there will be cobwebs around her as she waits for her big payday from Obama.

We cannot let our black constituency who think we run things start to observe:

A white man runs the State Department.

A white man is in charge of the Treasury.

A white man is in charge of the military.

A white-Hispanic (thanks George Zimmerman) man is in charge of housing and urban development.

A white man is in charge of Education.

A white woman is in charge of the Treasury.

A white man is in charge of Agriculture.

A white man advises Obama on national security.

A white man is even in charge of the CIA! What? Obama can't trust a black person with any secrets?

The only blacks with cabinet rank are Eric Holder (Justice – putting people in jail), Lisa Jackson (Environmental Protection Agency), Ron Kirk (U.S. Trade Representative), Jeh Johnson (recently put in charge of DHS) and Susan Rice (former UN Ambassador).

Five blacks of twenty-two people in Obama's cabinet.

And Holy Mother of Katrina, Obama put a white man in charge of the Federal Emergency Management Agency (FEMA).

To be fair, Obama never claimed that blacks would run things after his election. He never even promised anything special to black people. But you as a black leader must keep the myth alive.

Obama's victory is our (vicarious) victory. It does not matter if he addresses black concerns or not. And you must not concern yourself with the insane and stupid concept of "accountability" as Tavis Smiley wrote about in his book *Accountable*:

"During the run-up to the 2008 presidential election, while I was still the resident political commentator on the Tom Joyner Morning Show, I caused quite a stir among the listeners, who are largely African-American, by insisting that we hold then Senator Barack Obama accountable for both his political record and his campaign promises. I wasn't singling him out, but rather applying the same standard to him that we should apply to all. I feel now, as I did then, that it is our responsibility as engages citizens to expect now-President Barack Obama to live up to the promises that made him an appealing candidate." [vii]

Remember, issues are for white folks, and feeling good is for black folks. We had to re-elect Obama to emotionally validate us. It also helped confirm your own "blackness" to your constituency.

Remember it was God put Obama in office, although you would have a hard time explaining where God was when George W. Bush was elected twice. God only elects Democrats, right? [viii]

The Numbers Mean Nothing

As discussed earlier, we must maintain that even though a tremendous number of white Americans voted for Obama, racism is waiting for black people out of the gate and the white man is out to get us. [ix]

Affecting change is not your concern. Distracting black people into feeling good, rather than think about real issues is your concern. Keep them feeling good, and you are guaranteed a following.

Fun Fact: When Barack Obama was a U.S. Senator, he campaigned for a white Democratic senatorial candidate Ben Cardin, who was the opponent of black Republican candidate Michael Steele.

Obama: *"Listen, I think it's great that the Republican Party has discovered black people. But here's the thing...you don't vote for somebody because of what they look like. You vote for somebody because of what they stand for."*[x]

Obama was not serious when he said that. That was "campaign talk."

We professional race baiters must *encourage* black people to judge by the color of skin, not by the content of character. Never say this publicly, but know that Dr. Martin Luther King, Jr. got it wrong.

CHAPTER 6

Black People Can Make It on Their Own

Despite evidence to the contrary, black people cannot make it on their own, and they should not believe their lying eyes.

The successful black Liberal Democrat Progressive authentically black leader (you) makes sure to drive this point home as a sure way to fun and profit.

"[M]any of today's liberals betray blacks by casting them all as the bearers of disadvantage and aggrievement whose end is not in sight. Like the old segregationist establishment, the new liberal racist one has black retainers including 'critics' such as the law professor Derrick Bell, the black historian Robin D. G. Kelley, and the political minstrel and street-theater impresario the Reverend Al Sharpton , who reinforce its illusions. They abet liberal racism by telling professional antiracist what they want to hear without expecting or effecting substantive change. Today's liberal racist establishment notoriously lacks the self-confidence and self-definition of its predecessors; what it wants...are ritual condemnations of its racism that implicitly credit its virtue.

"Those who know how to deliver such condemnations profit handsomely. It is one thing to defend a community that has developed a distinct identity in

oppression. It is another to foresee a Sisyphean struggle against racism that will never end. 'Racism is an integral, permanent, and indestructible component of this society,' writes Derrick Bell. The blackness he, Kelley, and Sharpton espouse is oppositional only, as if they were saying, 'I am excluded; therefore, I am.' Full inclusion would bring their implosion. So would full exclusion, of course; so they strike evasive, sometimes ingratiating poses of dignity-in adversity, resisting inclusion just gently and sorrowfully enough to make white liberals uneasy and eager to offer support. Playing this game involves finding racism in every leaf that falls while relying on reservoirs of white racial guilt and deference whose existence black racists deny even as they accept media pulpits, book royalties, academic tenure, and constitutional protections.

"Nice work, if you can get it—and skilled race pros certainly do." [i]

The lesson here is no matter the black icon, there is an evil white person who helped them to get to where they are and who is profiting off the efforts of said black icon.

Michael Jordan would be an unknown streetballer had it not been for Dean Smith, right?

And what of Oprah Winfrey, who credited her white male discoverer on one of her TV shows. Is it any guess that the man who started her career was an evil white racist?

Now that Tiger Woods knows he is black, let's examine his life. In a word…*Nike.*

Look at all the money that Nike is making off Tiger Woods. Without Woods, Nike would be Keds.

Whites have allowed these few black examples, just to give the *appearance* that black people can make it. The reality is, for the average black it is quite frankly too much work to overcome the oppression of America. And in the end, it is the white man who benefits the most.

Indoctrination replaces education, ergo critical thinking.

Accountability and personal responsibility have no place in black communities. Those are white values.

Black people must not believe that those who live in horrible conditions have made bad choices, because of bad values, and thus have bad character. It is always solely the fault of the white man, especially the Republicans, a common theme we have attempted to drive home in this book.

When you run out of ideas to remind black people that they can't help themselves, be sure to remember your safety net: *Government.*

You must teach black people that despite bad choices, their life situations are not their fault. Someone (white) is accountable, and this is why governments are formed; to allay the responsibilities of the misguided.

Blacks must always demand that the federal, state, county, and city governments take the responsibility of solving all the problems of the black community. It is the government's responsibility to provide jobs — not that we really expect some black people to work in the first place. It's much more lucrative for us to have black people sit around and pick up a check at their convenience, than to work.

A work ethic builds character, and it's a slippery slope to independence from there. We will have none of that.

That said, we will still demand government should have a cushy job ready, knowing that government can't create jobs. Our job is to act like we can, and "try."

The good news for us is government will maintain high unemployment in the black community, so blacks can complain that the jobs are going to (repeat with me)…*white people.*

ObamaCare: The Cure for all Ills?

ObamaCare is a perfect example of race pimping done spectacularly. Black people believe government must provide healthcare, because they have been taught to believe that government is awesome. [1]

In passing Obamacare, it was important that black people want what the *government* defines as good healthcare *insurance*, and not what other white people actually get: *fantastic* health *care*.

Despite the horrible rollout of Obamacare, the increased costs, the lack of doctors or even hospitals accepting the insurance, black people feel vindicated. They were told that the white man will pay for this, so it has to be good.

Ironically, black people aren't getting better healthcare. But that's not the point, as they *believe* that we have their best interest in mind.

In actuality, black people still go to substandard hospitals, wait in long lines behind illegal immigrants, and are treated like non-citizens, as there simply isn't enough health *care* to go around. But at least they have insurance, right!?

So just parade the occasional lucky few around who will receive treatment like championship rings, thus continuing the ruse. They won't know what hit them, until they have settled for pig feet, while you continue to eat pork tenderloin.

As you can see, we've left out nothing. We touch more on this in Chapter 10: *Promise Everything, Deliver Nothing.*

***

Dependence-thinking black people are easily led, and you teach them not to rock the boat. If on the small chance there are complaints, there is an easy and time-tested solution: Throw them a few more dollars.

The good news is you won't need much.

Even better news is despite ObamaCare, the mortality rate among blacks is high, so you don't have to put up with them very long.

There is also lots of black-on-black crime, but there is no reason to bring this up. And as you learned earlier, it's best to just dismiss this type of information.

If you are questioned about crime, simply tell your people that you will put more cops on the street. Funny how that works, even when black people say things like, "Kill the cops!"

Explain that you want them to have safe neighborhoods. They will believe you, because you are authentically black, and you have established credibility by doing absolutely nothing for them.

Black men will continue to fill the jails, because we have built in the conveyor belt. Say things like, "Incarceration rates of black men is a crisis!", knowing there is opportunity in crisis that you are helping to create.

"Baby Daddy" Syndrome – Thank God for White Feminists

America has a crisis, and it's "Baby Daddy" syndrome. That crisis is affecting young black men harshly, as prison population with young black men has been well documented. What has been overlooked for the most part however, is the lesser seen crisis is on black women.

It has been said that black women are angry. I'm inclined to agree. That said, if black women are angry, they have a right to be.

White feminists are feasting in America in comparison to black woman.

White feminist icons are married, have great jobs, or make $200,000 or more a speech, as feminist Hillary Clinton "earns." Meanwhile, their melanin-rich sisters are robbing Juwan to pay Jamaal, because they don't have husbands or even significant-others in their lives.

And when black Liberal women do have men, the men are ignorant thugs who have no idea of how to be real men.

I'm not going to bother pointing you to links about the black family. Suffice it to say that single women are running most families in the black community. Generations of young black women who don't know what it means to be "Daddy's little girl."

Liberalism doesn't create black warriors or princesses, but instead creates pimp and pole-dancers.

Do you see the potential!

Single black women will have needs for quite some time, and will help you to train your future generation of dependents, save their proficiency at killing in the womb. [ii]

But don't be dismayed.

If for some reason we happen to run out of blacks, we will be able to apply our trade to the Mexicans with little disruptions. Plans are already underway for our next edition in this "How To" series:

How to be a Race Pimp for Fun and Profit…even if you're an illegal Mexican.

How do we control blacks who want to think for themselves? It's simple.

We cannot allow black people to live outside the zones we've established for their "care." Black people are easier to control when they congregate in public housing, or the projects, government housing.

You know what…we're friends now, so let's just be honest and call public housing what it really is…the ghetto.

Every ghetto need ghetto schools; government school.

It is the government's responsibility to keep spending money on schools, even if they don't perform.

Remember this: lack of money is the only reason why black children are not getting a good education, is it not?

So what teachers and administrators alter test scores and graduate kids who can't read? Tell your people, these are acts of love, meant to level the playing field; so black kids can compete with their non-black counterparts…in the real world.

How do you make all this work?

Pay attention! Highlight this part if necessary: Corral your black people in these urban occupation centers.

Big cities are not just so white people can catch a play uptown and have dinner out with the spouse. Cities allow us to provide group-thought for black people.

We bombard the airwaves with what our people want to hear, "urban." Blacks huddle together in groups, and don't allow "white" thought to penetrate, with our help of course.

If there are malcontents, like black Conservatives—easier to spot than a kangaroo in a dinner jacket—you banished them. Send those sellouts to the suburbs to live as Uncle Toms and Step-n-Fetchits among the evil white folks.

Meanwhile, you are firmly in control of the ghetto.

Understand that you will experience problems with poverty, crime, gangs, and lack of urban development. But you will have a black mayor, a black congressman, a black city manager, a black superintendent of schools, a black county treasurer, a black chief of police, a black fire chief, blacks on the county Board of Supervisors, blacks on the school board, etc. who will be more than willing to listen and try.

You will need to find ONE white man, preferably a Republican to blame for all those problems. If a white Republican doesn't exist, don't be afraid to refurbish one. Blame Republican Presidents George W. Bush, Ronald Reagan, Herbert Hoover, or T.R. Roosevelt.

The Immigrant Problem

Immigrants who find success in America are "parasites." Don't be fooled by claims of "hard work" and "the dream to do better here than in their own country."

Immigrants are racists too, sent here to help the white man continue paralyzing the black community. Everyone is against black folks.

These immigrants have been passing up black folks economically, and nobody seems to recognize the inequities. Immigrant black Africans don't seem to have the spines to become victims. They are not really black because they are not ghetto.

Note: Ghetto = Authentically Black, always.

Black Africans embarrass black Americans as they immigrate here legally by the thousands, outperforming indigenous blacks. Those black Africans should be ashamed of themselves, choosing success above victimhood.

They don't know their place, which upsets our white Democratic liberal benefactors who get offended when blacks think they can get along without them. They are creating too many successful examples, and that my friend is a threat.

How do we get around this?

Claim that the government had some "program" to make those Africans successful. You must at all times say that Amerikkka is a horrible place for blacks to try to succeed, regardless of the success of immigrant black Africans here.

Never encourage hard work, and please never let them know that blacks after slavery believed in hard work and did not depend on the government for their existence. Immigrants are racists, including black immigrants. If anyone challenges you, don't forget that sweet cry of "Racism!"

[1] Except for the police.

CHAPTER 7

Be "Tolerant," but Never Tolerate Diversity

There is tolerance, and there is tolerance. See the difference?

The key to tolerance is acting tolerant. For example, never tolerate the use of the word "nigger" by whites. [1] This is the fastest way to prove your tolerance and political correctness.

You can go a step further by not allowing words that sound like "nigger" such as the non-race based word "niggardly [i]," defined as "grudgingly mean about spending."

When you hear these things, you must boycott, picket, hold press conferences, demand firings, ask for hearings, and even demand reparations.

What is tantamount in this example is to deflect from the fact that the person offended by the use of the word "niggardly" was ignorant of its meaning. [2] We can't have people noticing how ignorant some of our people are, because that's our secret. (See Chapter 12: Whatever you do, don't educate black people).

Never scold your own people for saying, "nigga," "nigger," or any such derivative, e.g. my nigga, niggarachi, and so on.

Saying "nigga" for black people is a part of blacks' tribal [3] language, which is why black people are the only ones allowed to say it. The word "nigga" bonds blacks. It is a reminder of what white racist Democrats used to call black people, and now blacks have taken the word back to denigrate themselves. It is important that black people always hold themselves to this lower standard.

As with all rules, there are exceptions.

If a wealthy, politically-connected white Democratic liberal, you want to support you financially says "nigger" publicly, like former KKK member and late Senator Robert Byrd did on national TV [ii], it is your duty to say he did not mean it in that racist Republican way.

"Imagine what would be said about a Republican appearing on Fox News Sunday, *talking about how his mother complained about 'white niggers.' Would a nationwide mea culpa tour be demanded, including detours to kiss the rings of Jesse Jackson and Al Sharpton, not to mention those who would be considered 'white niggers' offended? As he was an old Democrat (age seems to be an excuse for exhibiting old ways of thinking), Byrd suffered no real repercussions from his verbal faux pas."*[iii]

"The ex-Klansman's admirers praise his historical knowledge, mastery of procedural rules, and outspokenness. They refer to the Senate's senior Democrat as the 'conscience of the Senate.' They downplay his white-sheet-wearing days as a 'brief mistake' — as if joining the Klan were like knocking over a glass of water. Oopsy." [iv]

There are many other examples, but I think you get the picture. Democrat good—even if he is a good-for-nothing racist scoundrel. Republican bad—even if he adopts black children and builds homes for single black mothers.

White racist Liberal Democrats can change and should always be given the benefit of the doubt [v]. White Republicans NEVER change; they are racists, yesterday, today, and forever.

Regardless of what color you are, you will soon be free to think of black Liberals as niggers, and actually get away with it.

***

A Bit of History on the Thought Police

The politicians of the defunct Union of Soviet Socialist Republics (USSR) got it right. They had a committee called the *Politburo* which was the chief policy making body of the Soviet Union. Also this committee did not tolerate deviation from the (Communist) "Party Line." The Soviets knew that freedom of thought would threaten their power. They created "gulags" [vi] for people, called dissidents, who dared to express such freedom of thought. The populations of that nation, as well of the satellite nations of the Soviet Union, knew they had to keep their feelings to themselves, or else find themselves arrested in the middle of the night and taken someplace far away from their families, maybe never to be seen or heard from again. Fear kept them in line.

You must take your lesson from history — *freedom of thought must never be encouraged.*

You must make other blacks afraid to openly express feelings other than your standard doctrine. Make them afraid to be called an "Uncle Tom." [4]

You are the Politburo in the black community; you set the party line. Only your opinion matters in the community. Yours is the only correct view. Black people must not be allowed to think for themselves. Black folks who dare to think for themselves are sellouts, traitors, and turncoats. Ban black independent thought and critical/rational thinking or you will lose control over them.

"But for a minority group like American blacks, whom history has left with a deep sense of vulnerability, shame becomes a primary means of reinforcing the group's story. Shame provides the muscle to keep individuals in line with group authority.

And shame does this muscling by making conformity to the group explanation the measure of one's love for the group. Thus noncomformity is a failure of love, a betrayal. And this is the most constant charge against the black conservative—that he does not love his own people—an unpardonable sin that justifies his symbolic annihilation." [vii]

"[W]e're supposed to fit into some kind of pre-defined box; we all know the drill by now. Black men aren't supposed to think for themselves. They're supposed to be for Leftist causes and issues, come hell or high water – and if we don't, if we question them, on any level whatsoever, then we're 'Juan Williams'd' – meaning thrown under the bus, tossed overboard, kicked to the curb. You get the idea." [viii]

"[Defend] O.J. Simpson, even though he was guilty and had distanced himself as far as possible from his blackness. It never considered that an even-handed consideration of the evidence and equanimity at a just outcome might both shame the devil and set a standard for excellence. No, blacks had to 'win'—that is, deprive whites of their preference. It defends Marion Barry, a corrupt crack-head mayoring a black city with a crack problem. Why? Because whites didn't like it. It believes Tawana Brawley, long past the point when any child gives up on Santa Claus. Why? Because she accused whites of hideous acts, the kind of thing they 'would do.' It prioritizes affirmative action above other goals, even though the black masses derive little benefit from it. Why? Because it disguises the elite black interest as the general black interest. And also, whites don't like it.

"The O.J.- and Barry - defenders are no different from the Founding Father worshippers. Anything 'black,' however odious, must be defended or denied,

and anything 'white' attacked or dismissed. George Washington's slave-mongering matters, but O.J. Simpson's wife-beating doesn't. David Duke's racism signifies, but not the Nation of Islam's. Racial profiling of blacks is wrong, but feel free to throw Arab Americans up against the wall. Tawana Brawley's inconsistencies mean nothing, those of a testifying cop, everything. Why? Because whites got away with gang-raping and torturing nigger gals for centuries—big deal, they finally had to pay for one. They've snickered publicly about railroading and murdering blacks since Reconstruction—so how they like O.J. getting away with murdering one of them....Poor man's justice—simply being able to stick it to someone else—is no justice at all. Payback lessens both the payor and the payee." [ix]

"There is little room in the Black community for freedom of expression, or for many of the other freedoms that Blacks demand from Whites. The Black community is run by an oligarchy of brownshirt plantation overseers who could improve their Nazi impersonations only if they spoke German. (Jawohl, Mein Schwartzefuehrer!—Authors) The Black brownshirts move in swiftly when any of the rank-and-file publicly stray. But it is in the defense of the Democratic Party that they are at their most vicious....And although they ridicule their own elitist leadership in private, they will attack anyone, Black or otherwise, who dares to say the same things in public." [x]

"The Black Politburo never misses an opportunity, however trivial, to conduct a thorough witch hunt of those blacks who persist in thinking for themselves. Even the most black-identified, Democrat-registered, affirmative-action-supporting black just surfing the Net and living his life is confronted daily with the knowledge that his 'leaders' are tyrants:

On Tom Joyner's extremely influential nationwide black radio show, R&B singer Brian McKnight found himself being grilled for having performed at the 2000 Republican National Convention. The powerful DJ vowed to lead a boycott against the singer's albums. 'I'm an entertainer, and it had nothing to do with politics," McKnight heretically said. Also, the DJ 'tried to make [my not voting] seem like I thought I was too good to vote. That was not it at all. Part of having the right to vote is having the right not to vote when you can't find a candidate that reflects your views.

Entertainer and movement stalwart Harry Belafonte is 'worried' about young black megastar Will Smith because of his lack of overt activism....Popular black actress Gabrielle Union grew up in a small white town and had a multicultural clique of friends but longed for black companionship. After enduring her high school classmates' ignorance (like dismissing her athleticism as natural to blacks), she made for the University of Nebraska, in part because of its large black student population. Once there she was immediately deemed not black enough. Hazed for having too many white friends, she transferred after one semester. Malcolm X's daughter had much the same experience." [xi]

Even black media personalities such as Tavis Smiley, who is far from being a "black Conservative," must be put in his place when he gets too independent from the rest of us. We must question his blackness and must accuse him of "Beating White Man's Drum of Nazi Superiority", as demonstrated here:

"Tavis Smiley Promotes CNN as 'caught in the middle real news, while pushing these frivolous white 'fact checks'-which never includes helpful facts for black news in the U.S. Let me break this Internet issue down for black people, before they start listening to Tavis Smiley and suffer yet another issue, that leaves blacks out in the cold due to 'black leaders' of this day & age. Tavis Smiley is yet another black man that doesn't get it." [xii]

So you see, critical thinking is for white people only, and black people should not want to be white:

"[T]he curricula in use in schools attended primarily by African American students are void of emphasis on critical thinking, reasoning, and logic. The failure to afford opportunities for African American students to develop

those essential skills is likely to contribute to their being referred and placed in special education at much higher rates than are White students, who are indeed provided with access to a rigorous curriculum and to gifted-and-talented programs." [xiii]

If black people start using logic, using critical thinking skills, instead of being emotional, they will most likely engage in self-reflection, which can only end badly for you.

Imagine the problems you will create if they become educated. Never confuse black folks by giving them facts.

There is nothing on earth meaner than a black Liberal who wakes from a stupor, especially when they wake up to facts. These people become black Conservatives, the most dangerous blacks of all to you. Consider the black Conservative your mortal enemy, worse than the KKK.

Black Conservatives are like the freedmen of the past. When freedmen interacted with slaves, the slaves got uppity. It doesn't take many freethinkers to turn the tide.

Take the lesson of Toussaint L'Overture, the Haitian slave who revolted and freed Haiti from the three super powers of the world. It was he, one man, who caused black Haitians to get the guts to fight for freedom. You do not want that type of rebellion on your hands.

[1] There is an exception

[2] Keeping blacks ignorant is covered in later chapters.

[3] You can say "tribal," because you're black.

[4] This lesson can be much more effective if delivered in Ebonics.

CHAPTER 8

Handling the Media

You must play the media like Niccolò Paganini played the violin. Done correctly, you can put this program on steroids and be considered a "legitimate" spokesperson for the black community.

Case in point: Sharpton

"[Al] Sharpton is 'a creature of the New York media,' Wilbert Tatum, publisher of New York's black newspaper, the Amsterdam News, *told* Newsday. *'When they saw Al Sharpton, who was articulate, fat and wore jogging suits, with a medallion around his neck and processed hair, they thought that he would be the kind of caricature of black leadership they could use effectively to editorialize without editorializing at all...While white media were using Al as a caricature, he was organizing the troops to do what respected black leadership could not do: speak to the issues without fear or favor, and use media in the process. Media thought they were using Al, and Al was using media."*[i]

Manipulate the Media

Of all the things you may do in your role as a black person suppressing other blacks, you must get all the media attention you can garner. Here is the process:

You need to get out press releases, on a daily basis if possible, to major media outlets, especially to the black media. You need to comment on the economy, domestic issues, foreign issues, the weather, and above all RACE.

If you can make the melting polar ice cap on Mars or the shifting of the earth's axis racial issues, then blame it on the white man, you are a master.

You need to make friends with black reporters from white and black media because they expect you to make good print and good sound bites for them. Always have your own photographer with you when you go to major events. Be photographed with movers and shakers, including future movers and shakers.

Get your own radio talk show. You want black callers to call in and talk about the white man constantly. It's the white man! It's the white man! It's the white man…*ad infinitum.*

Get a column in a newspaper and write about RACE.

Get a blog and blog about RACE.

Get listed in media publications as an expert on RACE.

Write books with titles like: *Don't You Dare Leave the Democratic Plantation* or *Black Power Gonna Git Yo Mama; Personal Responsibility is for White Folks; It's All the White Man's Fault; If it Ain't Ghetto, It Ain't Black; The Joy of Victimhood; Critical Thinking is for White Folks; Being on Time is for White Folks;* and *The White Man Owes Me: How to Get Your 40 Acres and a Lexus.*

Whenever you are interviewed, remember, you represent *The Authentic Black Point of View.* It doesn't matter that you can't gather enough black people together to throw a decent house party or that more people saw your kid's 3rd grade play. The media will help you by filming at angles that make your crowd of 20 look like 5000, and they will report it that; because you're a black leader. Excuse me…a *legitimate* black leader.

You can bolster the concept that you represent the authentic black point of view by using your litany of failures in life as a badge of honor.

"Remember, when I ran for [insert losing political run here], I represented hundreds of thousands of my constituents' points of view."

In the black world, it isn't what you accomplished that matters; it's that you *tried.*

It's not your lack of a track record; it is your "good intentions."

Just say, *"I have always been down for my people."*

It is important that you Establish Your Street "Cred"

You must take a controversial stance in support of lunacy.

For example, when a theatre owner is made to pay $80,000 to black people whom he "offended" by asking them to silence their cell phones and their mouths, you must support this, saying that the theater owner got what he deserved. He was trying to limit the civil rights of black people to be as disruptive as newborns at the theater or anywhere else.

If you are later challenged on your stance, quickly say that your comments were taken out of context. Even better, blame the racist white Republican conservative establishment for trying to distort your message.

Accuse them of always trying to get you and to take you down. You must be the consummate victim, and white people the consummate oppressors.

Always be ready to help those already in the spotlight.

When a prominent black entertainer dies, be at the ready to make a political statement where none is needed. Stir up controversy about some white man trying to steal the entertainer's legacy. The objective is just to be seen, because your black people will believe you are prominent, though you add little or nothing to add to the event.

When a black entertainer, e.g. a rapper is caught in a crime, look directly into any camera and blame slavery, poverty, family abuse, and above all *racism* for his or her predicament. It certainly is not the entertainer's fault. The white man *made* them that way. He or she is only the victim, and the impact of racism made them do it.

If that artist is very prominent, claim that the white man is trying to bring him down, even if there are no white men to be found. Surely there is one white man involved, like the cop, the judge, and so on.

Tip: Whatever you do, don't go to bat for a black entertainer who is not "down" with the folks, if you know what I mean. If a black entertainer is not doing gangsta rap, or involved in an activity that can raise your street cred, simply monitor the situation, and evaluate for potential gain at a later date.

Another "hip pocket" media ploy is to publicly attack symbols of white supremacist past, even if the object has no tie to white supremacy, like the confederate flag. This tactic is always good for headlines, and generally allows you to ignore the real issues that you don't want to take on anyway.

Remember the brouhaha when Georgia officials approved a specialty license plate featuring the Confederate flag? I do.

It reminded me that black Liberals are easier to train than children. Ring certain bells and they salivate like Pavlov's dogs.

Georgia officials approved a specialty license plate that features the Confederate battle flag. How long do you think it took for the "civil rights advocates" to end their tea break?

Don't expect these race pimps to get upset about the black people killing other blacks, when there is a license plate to picket!

The claim is that the license plate is a reminder of slavery, Jim Crow, and the Klan…all Democrat institutions.

What race baiting black Liberals want is the complete white-washing of white Southerners' past. Forget your history, abandon your heritage, because any part of it is tainted in today's politically correct world.

The Catholic church had the Crusades, Germany gassed the Jews, and so on. For blacks, no harm no foul, at least not when there are Southerners trying to be proud of their heritage.

Not knowing one's heritage can allow you to create whatever you background choose. It's convenient for Liberal blacks to forget that Africans were sold into slavery…by other Africans. And nothing has changed.

Modern-day slavery black slave owners — black Liberal "leaders" like the Congressional Black Caucus (CBC) — are the new Anthony Johnson's. [1]

The CBC sells more blacks into slavery than all the African tribes combined.

Blacks seem to be proud of this heritage of blacks selling other blacks, embracing "African" in front of American, though 99.9 percent of blacks have never been to African and can't tell you from what tribe they descend.

Southern Christian Leadership Conference spokesman Maynard Eaton said of the new GA license plate:

"To display this is reprehensible...We don't have license plates saying 'Black Power.'"

Just to be clear, this license plate doesn't say "White Power," though Eaton would certainly love for people to imply that. While on the subject of Black v White, here is a short list of what Maynard doesn't feel is reprehensible:

- The Congressional Black Caucus
- Black Entertainment Television
- Black Liberation Theology
- Black employee unions (associations)
- The NAACP
- Historically Black Colleges and Universities
- A half-white president who claims nothing except his blackness!

And let's not forget black holes, black ink, black toner, black coffee, and black magic.

Truth be told, except for the racist Southern Democrats, the average Southerner has no concern with oppressing black people. They understand what black ball players have done for the SEC sports programs, and enjoy the shared heritage of soul food and Southern cooking.

But there is money in this license plate, which is why we must take issue!

The indisputable fact is, black people have much larger issues to worry about, than a flag on a license plate.

I'd say the biggest problem in the black [Liberal] community is having to support the most worthless president in history. This black president who has done more harm to the black community than all the circa 1860 and circa 1960 Southern racist Democrats combined, and 1000 license plates. But that's our secret.

There is no money in solutions, so avoid boring the media by talking about solutions to problems.

Who wants to hear about "solutions?" Keep them wondering what you will do next. (See *How to Run an Effective Boycott*)

Constantly make big threats to the media about "all hell breaking loose," "bloodshed," and brothers and sisters "finding freedom at home."

Throw in "Burn, baby burn!" for good measure. None of it has to make sense, which is why this tactic is so cool.

Have a press conference and make big demands. Say if those demands are not met by a certain deadline, there will be serious consequences:

"In 1990, at a 'state of the inner city' press conference at city hall, [Michael] McGee —then a Milwaukee alderman—announced his intention to create the Black Panther Militia unless the problems of the inner city improved. He sought to enlist street gangs in the militia and provide them with weapons training. 'They can fight and they already know how to shoot,' he said. 'I'm going to give them a cause to die for.' By 1995, McGee threatened, the militia would carry out violent attacks in the city against "the government, the big private interests, the multi-millionaires."[ii]

It's appropriate to bug out your eyes here, and tilt your head. Be sure to look directly into the camera, if doing TV.

For extra points try to work in something about reparations, as this makes for great sound bites within the black community. By mentioning reparations, you imply that you are working for your people; it keeps them wondering when they will receive their checks. By the time they figure out there are no reparations, *you* will have cashed lots of checks.

Media provides an opportunity to drive home tried and true memes, so you cannot pass up these opportunities to double down. So when you are dealing with the media, regardless of the topic, accuse the government of constantly attacking your constituency and keeping them in poverty. Remind people of how many houses some white Republican owns, or how much money they made last year from Big Oil.

Clichés work. *Big Tobacco is killing black people.*

If the Republicans don't want to raise the debt ceiling, say that they want to keep black people in poverty. It makes sense. If the government can't print or spend more money, then black people will suffer. Who cares that white people will suffer too? Nobody will be thinking about that.

Black people's suffering easily trumps white people's suffering (as it should). And since you are actually vying for one of the coveted spots to become a punisher, you must make sure that the message stays on point. This way black people will find you likable and genuine and white people will fear you.

With media, you will have good days and bad days, and we want to prevent bad days from happening. Usually bad days are when you are caught off guard on a topic. The expectation is not for you to be an expert in all topics, just that you "represent" for blacks, so that you can get to your payday as expeditiously as possible.

The Panic Button

If for any reason you are stumped during a media appearance, you have a panic button: Cry "Racism!" We alluded to this throughout this book; however here is the title of a blog posting that illustrates the point most effectively: *"White Woman Gets Raped by A Black Man and It's the White Man's Fault!"* [iii]

Racism works in all circumstances. In this example racism was used to try to exonerate black teens from a hate crime:

"*African American youth are disadvantaged from birth and their aggressive behavior is an outward manifestation of righteous black rage and should be understood as such. They were taken by force from mother Africa by unscrupulous tribes under consignment from the white colonialists. While slaves in the African diaspora stranded in America, they are bombarded by the media controlled by Zionist aggressors. Please be understanding of my brothers and sisters.*" [iv]

Bonus: Media sound bite for this example: "*Had these black youth received reparations, they would not have had so much pent up rage. America should be ashamed!*"

It makes sense, as long as you don't try to make sense of what you see?

When doing black radio talk shows, announce that the main problem in the black community is racism, especially the racist Republicans. Say you are trying to get black folks to wake up. Exaggerate instances of racism.

For example, if there was black voter suppression in one election, for the next election, plan on mentioning unconfirmed reports of voter suppression in several states. Nobody will check you out, for fear of being called racists. The media will not hold you responsible for hearsay, and your constituency will love you for your "honest" vigilance. Besides, those comments will likely be forgotten. If not, at least you planted the seeds of suspicion. [v]

We touched on this earlier in the publication, but it bears repeating. Sometimes you do need to let sleeping dogs lie. In other words, don't report everything.

"*Early this year, a white couple was carjacked, tortured, raped, and murdered by a group of black thugs. Christopher Newsom (23) was gang-raped, shot and set on fire. There are unconfirmed reports that the killers cut off his penis while he was still alive. The going-to-straight-to-hell murderers made Channon Christian (21) watch, and then they gang-raped her over four days and left her to die. There are unconfirmed reports that her breasts were cut off while she was still alive. ...I've noticed that mainstream media are reluctant to report this story, especially when it first happened. In light of the blanket coverage the Duke 'rape' case received, the paucity of coverage in this case seems a bit unbalanced. I mean, isn't the brutal, black-on-white gang-rape, mutilation, and murder of two people more than or at least as newsworthy as a white-on-black gang-rape (which obviously was phony)? Even if the stripper's allegations had been true, why was the Duke case burning up the airwaves while the Christian-Newsom case barely emits a spark?*" [vi]

As you can see, you must be selective on bringing attention to overt cases of racism. As the above case and the next prove, there are some cases where it behooves you to ignore media comment completely as in the case made against Planned Parenthood:

"*Several black and Hispanic male employees of Planned Parenthood of Los Angeles have filed multiple complaints of racism against the organization, charging they were the subject of constant slurs in a hostile, anti-male environment controlled by white women.*

"*The employees made the allegations in sworn affidavits filed with California's Equal Employment Opportunity Commission, or EEOC, and Fair Employment & Housing Administration, or FEHA.*

"*According to an EEOC affidavit filed by employee Nnamdi Nkwuda, a member of Planned Parenthood's management 'used the word nigger directed to me.*'" [vii]

There were no protests from our high-profile black leaders at all. Why? Because it was not a white conservative company or organization involved. It was Planned Parenthood, a friend to the liberal white and black establishment. Planned Parenthood has purchased the right to say "nigger" as much as they want. What power! Soon you too may possess such power.

[1] Anthony Johnson was the first slave owner and he was black.

CHAPTER 9

Going on the Offensive & the Dreaded Black Conservative

"One more word, soul brother. You had it made. Black folks would have followed you anywhere. You could've been another Marcus Garvey or even another Malcolm X. But instead you ain't nothin' but a pimp with a chicken-shit backbone."
— "Gravedigger" Jones from the film *Cotton Comes to Harlem*

The best defense is a good offense when attacked. The most successful (wealthiest) black Liberal profiteers call any white person who criticizes them or their black friends a Nazi, Klan member, Aryan Nations member, cracker, Dixiecrat, honky conservative, or just a plain old white supremacist. This guarantees you room to maneuver, should you later need a little elbow room to throw blows.

Recently Charlie Rangel called Conservatives "confederates," and you can learn from this. Note the deft reference to slavery without actually saying the word "slavery."

Genius! You should be marking this area of the text for later use.

Rangel used this tactic because Conservatives were for shutting down the government and reining in spending. If Conservatives rein in spending, then how will Rangel get paid?!

Rangel's gambit was an excellent tactic against the typical Conservative. This is because Conservatives have been trained *not* to fight; to take the high ground. You can and should always use this to your favor. Are the Conservatives racists or any of the things you might call them? Of course not, Silly!

But you should have learned by now, that the truth doesn't matter. It is what you can convince people to think about themselves, and get others to adopt as truth.

The good news is you don't have to do this all on your own; there is lots of help.

White Liberals will continue to feel guilty for some time. Be warned however. There is a group who has the potential to throw a wrench in your gears and expose the game. This is the dreaded black Conservative.

These people are the **Amos 'n' Andy-ers, Aunt Jemimas, backstabbers, behind scratchers, big-shot-coons,** black-anglo-saxons, **black stooges,** boot-lickers, **bought-and-solds, bourgies,** brown pelicans, **buck-dancers, bug-eyes,** Buckwheats, **butt-kissers, caste flunkies, chicken-eaters, co-**caucasians, **cocktail-sippers,** coconuts, **cotton pickers, de-blackeds,** fades, Farinas, **foot shufflers, hafricans,** handkerchief-head Negroes, **hi yallers, homey-kindas,** *homo Tomus americanuses,* **house boys,** house Negroes, **howdy-doodies,** hyenas, **integratins, inauthentics, jigaboos, Judases, Kingfishers, knee-shakers, lawn jockeys, low-belly-creepers, me-too-bosses,** opporTOMists, Oreo ™ cookies, parasites, **pleaser-and-appeasers,** porch monkeys, **prefabrications,** race traitors, **rent-a-Toms,** Rev. Pork Chops, Sambos, servants-of-the-right-wing, self-haters, self-loathers, sellouts, **slap happies, shifty-eyes, shoeshine boys, skunks, snow-blacks, speak-when-spoken-tos,** Stepin Fetchits, **stooges,** Stymies, sugarcanes, **thank-ya-bosses, Thomasinas, tomfools,** tools of the white man, **tree-tops,** Trojan Horses, **turncoats, turn-the-other-cheeks,** wannabes, weasels, wombats, **un-colas, uppities,** Uncle Remuses,, Uncle

Ruckuses, Uncle Toms, wannabe whites, **waterboys, white-breads, white-wardly-mobiles,** whitewashes, **window dressers, wooly-heads, zebras, and zip-coons who want to ruin your future.**

Commit these pejoratives to memory, so we can avoid overuse (and misuse) of Uncle Tom.

"Black women were the first to use the term[Uncle Tom] to describe Black men who left the Republican Party to join the Democratic Party. The Honorable Marcus Garvey (was) the first public figure to call Black Democrats Uncle Tom's. As a matter of fact, one of the best known figures that Garvey called an Uncle Tom was W.E.B. Dubois. Dubois was very critical of the 'Back to Africa' (movement) led by Garvey's United Negro Improvement Association (UNIA). Garvey called Dubois an 'Uncle Tom.' Dubois responded by calling Garvey 'the most dangerous Black man in America.' Garvey followed with calling Dubois 'purely and simply a white man's nigger...') [1] The most unusual phenomenon about the term 'Uncle Tom' is that it is currently directed to Black Republicans and not to Black Democrats, even though the ideas of these Black Republicans have not changed since the abolition of slavery." [i]

Black Conservatives for the most part are thick-skinned and well-educated, thus they can and will present major problems for you. They *must* be silenced as quickly as possible.

Sometimes the best tactic is to ignore them.

If you can marginalize them, then perhaps they won't gain a voice. After all, the system is against them as well, and they have to fight not only our scheme, but many times they battle their own just as hard.

Another tactic that works with the "urban" or "hip" black Conservatives is to simply denigrate them to other blacks. This group still has hopes of being popular within the black community, as they feel a connection to "blackness." They try to keep their foot in the door, bouncing back and forth between issues. They call themselves Conservatives, but they really are not. They are remnants of our good work in destroying the black community, and can easily be brought back into the ranks. Their constant want for approval in the black community is their downfall.

Ad hominem attacks such as ridiculing black Conservatives' names is yet another good tactic. I know it sounds silly, but remember the denominator you are working with not exactly the brightest bulbs in the box. They LOVE creative name-calling.

For example, if one has the name Ezola, call her "Ebola." [ii]

Condoleezza becomes "Condemnesia" or as "Reverend" Jeremiah Wright called Rice, "Condoskeeza." And Condoleeza isn't even a Conservative, but unquestionably a Republican in name only.

Publicly accuse the feet-shuffling, sellout, disrespectful, self-hating Uncle Tom or Aunt Jemima, Stepin Fetchit, sycophant, extremist, and persona-non-grata blacks who call themselves "conservatives" and who oppose you of being self-serving house-negro whores of the white establishment.

Note the effusive use of adjectives to describe this person. This type of grandiose description can be quite effective, if for no other reason than to train your people not want to mess with you.

If a black Conservative calls you out on any facts you cannot dispute, your retort is "White folks paying you to say all that?" in hopes of embarrassing them. Understand that this will only buy you a little time, and you will need to employ additional tactics.

Accuse black Conservatives of having Messianic complexes and delusions of grandeur while saying, "Yassa Massah! We's good black folks. We sho' gonna do whate'r yall say!" to their white puppet masters.

Tell your constituency these sellouts are the "enemy within," and they must be exposed and opposed vigorously.

It is your duty to isolate them. Tell them how "not black" they are, and compare them to a black nerd like Steve "Did I do that?" Urkel, or worse yet, a white nerd like Gomer Pyle.

Your people must always question the black Conservative's *blackness*. This is a lesson not to the black Conservative, but to black people watching the charade. Your constituency must know that to deviate from your standard doctrines is to "work against the black race" and is contributing to their genocide. You, the Black Politburo, are reminding them that dissent within the black community will not be tolerated. Don't worry; your people will still consider you to be tolerant.

[1] Presumably Garvey slammed Dubois in that fashion because Dubois was the only Black officer of the NAACP at the time.

CHAPTER 10

Promise Everything, Deliver Nothing

"If you wish to be a success in the world, promise everything, deliver nothing."
— Napoleon Bonaparte

Dealing with blacks is not the same as dealing with Jews, for example. Jews will hold your feet to the fire. With blacks Liberals however, it is like negotiating for tricking a third-grader.

Black Liberal politicians sell out for pennies on the dollar, and their black constituents get what amounts to bubble gum machines prizes. In other words, you get them cheap!

The Case for Reparations

If you can inspire your constituency to read books like *I Love My Chains: Why I Refuse to Leave the Plantation*, consider yourself a success. A reparations advocate emailed one of the authors of this book:

"Why is it that every time we Reparationists challenge this government and the corporations that profited from slave labor, that we get so much opposition to our strategies? The Reparations Movement is a global movement made up of reparations groups all throughout the world. We Reparationists in America are focused mainly on this continent because that is our historical reality. Reparations is about repair of structural inequities, repair of social systems, our political systems, our educational systems, our health systems, our cultural systems and our economic systems. To do that it will take billions of dollars. Just keep in mind that reparations is about repairing a people that had their existence altered through violations of their human rights. I still have a slave name. I still go to a slave school. I still practice a slave religion. and I still have ties to the global plantation even though 'they' say we are free. Lastly, Africa is in the last stage of Imperialism.

Reparations present so many money-making opportunities, as there is the hope of something for nothing. Though there are no black people alive today who were slaves, and no whites who were slave masters, black Liberals still want their 40 acres and a mule that the Democrats took away. In their angst lies opportunity.

The fact is that black people will never receive reparations, but let's keep that a secret as long as we can. Because we can make black anger pay off.

Here's the scam.

Book meetings in black churches and community centers, and do a two-hour lecture on the evils of slavery. [1] Provide details on how white slave owners and overseers tortured and brutalized their slaves. If you have to, make up fictional details, because people will love the drama of it all. The more horrible the situation, the better, as your objective is to make your black audience (potential money-makers) very emotional and angry.

Tell them those slaves were never paid for their labor, therefore your black audience—all descendents of those slaves— are owed back wages. Explain that the U.S. Government owes each of them $500,000. Get them excited about that.

Next, tell them you will send a claim on their behalf to the U.S. Government –for a legal handling fee of $50. They will be happy to fork over to you their cash. You will get your reparations from your own black people guaranteed, as Fox News Contributor and racial apologist Juan Williams writes of such a "reparatory entrepreneur" who made that exact scheme work:

[Attorney and "Father of Reparations"] Robert Brock, who for years barnstormed through the South making speeches at small black churches offering to file tax forms claiming $500,000 in reparations payments for individual black people if they first paid him a fifty-dollar fee. He made reparations for slavery the answer to every conspiracy theory launched against black people. He particularly blamed Jews and Hispanics and Arabs for the problems of black people, and announced that he was in agreement with white separatists who wanted blacks to go back to Africa. As crazy as all that seems, Brock got 165,000 people to hand over fifty dollars before the government caught up with him.[i]

Also when it comes to reparations, always talk about general terms and do not bother about details with logistics because logical thinking about the subject will raise too many questions among your constituency.

There are those who advocate cash payments directly to blacks. Should this to be a one-time payment or is it annuitized for a certain period of time or for life?

If you decide on some general fund for education, internal infrastructure, etc., how will you handle the backlash from those who believe they deserved individual payments? (Think of the people who gave Robert Brock $50 to get $500,000.)

Suppose a black person cannot prove slave ancestry? What does he or she get? Suppose a black person, such as the late grandmother of one of the authors or Carol Channing, who can pass for white, can prove slave ancestry? Is that person "black enough" to get reparations?

How would the dark-skinned blacks who cannot prove their slave ancestry feel when ancestry-verified blacks who can pass for white get reparations? There is going to be some violence in the reparations office.

How about the ones who lived as whites who did not suffer any kind of racism?

Do wealthy blacks like Oprah Winfrey, Robert Johnson of BET, Bill Cosby, and so on get reparations too?

Also, what about mixed race blacks?

Does someone like Lenny Kravitz, Halle Berry, Alicia Keys, or Jasmine Guy who are half-white get half the reparation money?

Does someone who has 25% slave ancestry get 25% of the reparation amount?

What about someone like the character in the Spike Lee joint *Bamboozled* who was 1/16th black [2] and appropriately named "1/16th black"?

Tiger Woods is mixed with several ethnic groups. Since he does not have 100% Black blood, what shall we do with him?

And does the "One Drop Rule" apply? How much black blood must you have to qualify for reparations?

What is the "one-drop-only" payment, a 40 of Colt 45 and an old Cadillac?

Believe it or not, there were free black slave owners in the South. Can their descendents claim slave ancestry, or do we say, "Sorry Charlie?"

Should the present-day families who were descended from the slavemasters be liable for reparations? Families such as the late Congressman Strom Thurmond's, Senator John McCain's, and Barack Obama's?

What about the descendents of slaves who actually fought for the Confederacy. Yes, they actually existed. Are these descendents disqualified because there were the "Uncle Toms" in the family? Or do they get 50% because the other side of the family supported the Union during the Civil War? [ii]

Do people who are considered "Uncle Toms" get reparations, i.e., Clarence Thomas?

What about the many descendents of American slaves who now live in Canada? Will they get the same reparations payment as American descendents of slaves, or do we ignore them, since they are Canadians?

Some ancestors only experienced slavery. Some of us have slave ancestors and lynched ancestors. Will we who have ancestors who were lynched get extra consideration added to our regular reparation check, like compensation for victims of violent crime?

Also will reparations in cash be ongoing because there will be more blacks born in the future?

Do blacks not even born yet deserve reparations?

That means there must be a payment system for every new black boy or girl born whose parents can prove slave ancestry. And it will be a permanent thing. Checks will be cut 24/7. [3]

Will there be systems in place to guard against fraud? There has been welfare fraud, Medicaid fraud, so there will be *reparations* fraud?

What about people such as parents and grandparents who are dead. They did not get reparations, so can we claim their share as ours too? Did they not deserve it too? Look at it as a legal inheritance.

Also too, if the U.S. Treasury dispenses reparations, does that not mean that the tax-paying native African immigrant, tax-paying black Caribbean immigrant, and tax-paying second generation blacks from those groups born here also contribute to those reparations? Is it fair to expect them to also pay to black Americans?

What fiduciary will be in charge of dispersing reparations payments? Who is to determine what trust company, bank, etc. will be in charge?

Who determines how much the payments will be? What criteria will be used that everyone involved with agree on, and will we all agree on the amount?

Suppose there are those who say that the payment is not enough? How will they be satisfied?

Suppose there are those who mismanage, squander their money away (and you know that will happen) and become flat broke? Are you prepared for their response when you say "Too bad. So sad. You blew it. Go away"?

After the check is signed will black people say, "Paid in Full" and not talk about what white folks did anymore?

Should any political entities that officially supported slavery be liable for reparations too?

There is a contention that reparations are also owed for years of segregation, particularly in the South. Is anything owed to the white Freedom Fighters who risked their lives and also died in the South at the hands of white supremacists?

Can you even imagine the amount of paperwork the government would generate on reparations?

These are questions you must avoid, but you can see how you can make the discussion of reparations fun...and PROFITABLE!

[1] ACORN or another government sham organization could easily find you grant money for this.

[2] 6.25% Black and 93.75% white "devil"

[3] Imagine reparation check cash advance businesses like paycheck cash advance businesses. Business will be booming.

CHAPTER 11

Support Radicals and their Causes

"Viva Fidel! Viva Che! Castro is the most honest and courageous politician I've ever met."
— Rev. Jesse Jackson, Sr.

If you really want to be a Liberal leader, you cannot appear to be part of the establishment. It is very important that you support radical leaders for "liberation." There is an added benefit to hanging out with radicals, as radicals can actually make you appear sane.

"Then there was the Rev. Jesse Jackson's 1993 trip to Nigeria, during which he lavished praise on military dictator Gen. Ibrahim Babangida as 'one of the great leader-servants of the modern world in our time.' This, I once observed in a story for Time *magazine, was the same Babangida who had ruthlessly suppressed political opponents, closed down independent newspapers, and allowed his country to become a major transshipment point for heroin and other illegal drugs to which millions of U.S. citizens are addicted. Was it a coincidence that after that effusive outburst, Babingida provided Jackson with a Nigerian Airways jet for a tour of southern Africa and encouraged his cronies to contribute hundreds of thousands of dollars to*

Jackson's causes in the U.S.?... [Nation of Islam Minister Louis] Farrakhan paid a visit during one stop on a whirlwind tour of tyrants. In addition to Abacha, whom he grandiloquently likened to Moses, Farrakhan praised the government of Sudan — which was then engaged (with Libyan support) in slaughtering thousands of people in a long-running civil war — for its 'wise Islamic leadership.' He then moved on to Iran — where he promised to help overthrow the "Great Satan," as the U.S. is known locally — and Iraq, where he voiced support for Saddam Hussein's fight against U.N. economic sanctions....The stated purpose of Farrakhan's junket was to find out for himself whether Western reports about totalitarian conditions in these benighted countries were true. But his real intent seems to have been to exonerate the regimes he sucked up to, in exchange for a potential big payoff.

"The clearest example was the praise he lavished on [Colonel Moammar] Qaddafi on a stop in Tripoli, (Libya) in exchange for which the Libyan dictator lavished him with a $250,000 human rights award and a promise of a $1 billion gift for his organization. Sadly for Farrakhan, the U.S. government would not allow him to accept either sum.

"At the time of Farrakhan's visit, Qaddafi was up to serious bad business in West Africa, where his protégés — Liberian President Charles Taylor and his ally, Sierra Leonean rebel Foday Sankoh — had instigated civil wars that led to the deaths of hundreds of thousands of people. Both Taylor and Sankoh — whose trademark tactic was to hack off the hands, arms and feet of his countrymen — had been trained, equipped and funded at Qaddafi's insurgency camps before being dispatched back to their countries. Qaddafi had blood all over his hands.

"Qaddafi's deep involvement in the genocidal conflicts in Liberia and Sierra Leone was no secret at the time of Farrakhan's visit. Since then, the evidence of his culpability has been front-page news as Taylor stands trial for human rights in an international court." [i]

You need to cozy up to third-world Marxist dictators with money and power; smoke cigars with them, and praise them for their leadership, no matter how much their people— including black people—are oppressed.

These people are also victims of white Amerikkkan criticism and their leaders deserve your support.

In case you're skeptical about this strategy, remember when Jesse Jackson met with Qaddafi to get the captors? This act made Jackson look good.

Also as a soon-to-be professional in the civil rights industry, you must be on the lookout for "right-wing" death threats or comments on assassination to foreign dictators who are not friendly to the United States ("The enemy of my enemy is my friend.")

A Black Man Confronts Africa *"makes it clear that [Africans] cannot look for help to American black leaders who fought so long and hard to achieve full civil rights for blacks in America and in South Africa. 'Weird things seem to happen to a lot of American black leaders when they venture into Africa,' he says. 'They go through a bizarre kind of metamorphosis when they set foot on the continent of their ancestors. Some of the most prominent veterans of America's civil rights wars—articulate advocates for human rights and basic freedoms for black people in America—seem to enter a kind of moral and intellectual black box when they get to Africa. Dictators are hailed as statesmen, unrepresentative governments are deemed democratic, corrupt regimes are praised for having fought off colonialism and brought about "development." Black Americans were most vocally at the forefront of calls for immediate democratic reform in South Africa, but when the subject turns to the lack of democracy and human rights elsewhere in Africa, those same black Americans become defensive, nervous and inarticulate.'*

"Richburg cites the example of Douglas Wilder, Virginia's first black governor since Reconstruction. When he asked Wilder what could be done to promote democracy in Africa, he got this reply: 'We cannot and should not force them to undergo a metamorphosis in seconds. If they are on track and on the path and giving evidence of trying to adjust, then our job is not to interfere and to understand that there is a difference from what they are accustomed to.' Richburg comments that if a white governor of a southern state had made such a statement about South Africa during the struggle to end apartheid, he would probably have been branded a racist 'and probably

by no less a personage than Doug Wilder.' The Reverend Louis Sullivan, author of the Sullivan Principles that were used to bring pressure on South Africa, told Richburg, 'We must be on the side of human rights and democracy. Many African leaders recognize it must be done and are trying to find a way to bring it about. I don't like to see anything stringent from America, saying you must do this or you must do that.'" [ii]

And let us not forget the "worker's paradise" of Cuba.

"Cuban Dictator Has Been One of the Most Prominent Enemies of the United States but He's Also Been an Untiring Supporter of Africans and African Americans... From the outset, Castro was one of the staunchest critics of American racism and the subordinate status of blacks... To the extent that figures like Castro consistently raised the issue of racism, they increased the pressure on the United States to support democracy and full equal rights for all its citizens." [iii]

Dictators are good, but black dictators are the bomb, my Negro!

You will learn to love these rabble-rousers for what they are—good people caught up in bad circumstances.

Trumpet black and Hispanic dictators not as bad men or despots, but as progressive democratic leaders and advocates of racial equality. Ignore the massive evidence to the contrary; that is for history to decide, not you.

In June 1984, Rev. Jesse Jackson accepted an invitation from one such rabble rouser, Fidel Castro to visit Cuba. Cuban writer Humberto Fontova reports:

*"'**Viva Fidel!**'bellowed Rev. Jesse Jackson during his speech at the University of Havana in June 1984, while trailing a 300 person entourage that included Rev. Jeremiah Wright. 'Viva Che Guevara!' he yelled again with fists raised high. 'Long live our cry of freedom!'*

"' He (Jesse Jackson) is a great personality,' reciprocated a beaming Fidel Castro, 'a brilliant man. Jackson's main characteristic is honesty.He is sincere and there is no hint of demagoguery in his speech.'

"*As mentioned, this was summer of 1984, so at the time, the world's longest-suffering black political prisoner suffered his incarceration and tortures in stoic defiance. 'Nigger!' taunted his jailers between tortures. 'We pulled you down from the trees and cut off your tail!'*

"*I do not refer to Nelson Mandela. No, this prisoner was being tortured a few miles away from the Revs. Jackson, Wright and their entourage of black American luminaries. The prisoner was a black Cuban named Eusebio Penalver and he was being tortured by Reverend Jackson's gracious hosts. Mr Penalver's incarceration and tortures stretched to 29 years which makes him* the longest-suffering black political prisoner in modern history, *surpassing Nelson Mandela's record in time behind bars and probably doubling the horrors suffered by Mandela during this period.*

"*Eusebio Penalver was bloodied in his fight with Castroism but unbowed for almost 30 years in its dungeons. He's what Castroites call a 'plantado'—a defiant one, an unbreakable one....Eusebio Penalver... spit in the face of his liar jailers. He scorned any 're-education' by his jailers. He knew it was they who desperately needed it. He refused to wear the uniform of a common criminal. He knew it was they who should do it. Charles Rangel, Jesse Jackson, Jeremiah Wright, Sheila Jackson Lee, Maxine Waters, Ron Dellums, etc. etc. etc. all toast his torturer. But through almost 30 years of those tortures Eusebio Penalver stood tall, proud and defiant.*

"*Shortly before his death in 2006, your humble servant here had the honor of interviewing Senor Penalver. 'For months I was naked in a 6 x 4 foot cell,' Eusebio recalled. 'That's 4 feet high, so you couldn't stand. But I felt a great freedom inside myself. I refused to commit spiritual suicide.'*

"Sr Penalver served several months of this 30 year sentence naked in a 'punishment cell' barely big enough to stand in, where he languished naked and in complete darkness. 'Castro's apologists, those who excuse or downplay his crimes — these people be they ignorant, stupid, mendacious whatever—they are accomplices in the bloody tyrant's crimes, accomplices in the most brutal and murderous regime in the hemisphere.'

"But have you ever heard of Eusebio Penalver? He became a U.S. citizen and lived in Miami for almost 20 years and would have been a cinch for the media to track down. Ever see a CNN interview with him? Ever see him on '60 Minutes'? Ever read about him in The New York Times? The Washington Post? The Boston Globe? Ever hear about him on NPR during Black History Month? Ever seen anything on him on the History Channel or A&E? Ever hear the NAACP or Congressional Black Caucus mention him?

"Why do I bother asking? He was a victim of the Left's premier pin-up boys...nuff said.

"The black Cuban doctor, Oscar Elias Biscet (an Amnesty International prisoner of conscience) presently suffers a sentence of 25 years in Castro's torture chambers essentially for saying things about Castro similar to what Nancy Pelosi, Bill Maher and Michael Moore made a career of saying about President Bush. Dr Biscet also denounced the Castro regime's policy of forced abortions. This latter 'crime' goes a long way towards explaining why you've never heard of him (and won't) in the MSM. For the record: President Bush awarded Dr Biscet the Presidential Medal of Freedom two years ago. (in a ceremony virtually blacked out by the MSM.)

"Today the prison population in Stalinist/Apartheid Cuba is 90% black while only 9% of the ruling Stalinist party is black. As the Congressional Black Caucus cavorted in Cuba recently, a black Cuban anti-communist named Antunez, who suffered 17 years in Castro's dungeons (essentially for quoting Martin Luther King and the U.N. Declaration of Human Rights in a public square), was on a hunger strike against Castroism. I will quote his sister from a samizdat smuggled out of Cuba last year while he was still in prison:

"'The Cuban government tries to fool the world with siren songs depicting racial equality in our country. But it is all a farce, as I and my family can attest, having suffered from the systematic racism directed at us by Castro's regime. My brother suffers the scourge of racial hatred every day. The beatings are always accompanied by racial epithets. They set dogs on him. They deny him medical attention. They kept him from attending his mother's funeral. The only thing I have to thank the Cuban revolution for,' she quoted her brother, 'is for restoring the yoke of slavery that my ancestors lived under.'

"VIVA FIDEL!— VIVA CHE GUEVARA!" (Jesse Jackson, June, 1984)" [iv]

"I wonder if Jackson would consider making a cause out of Dr. Óscar Elías Biscet. He is the Afro-Cuban physician and democracy leader who has been in the Castros' dungeons for a very long time. His models are Gandhi and Martin Luther King. George W. Bush gave him the Presidential Medal of Freedom (of course). (Biscet, somehow, didn't show up to accept.)

"Do you think Jackson would ever take an interest in him? That would surprise me. I think Jackson's — and the American Left's — attachment to, and affection for, the Communist dictatorship in Cuba is simply too great." [v]

"The Revs. Jesse Jackson and Al Sharpton along with leaders in the NAACP and our other civil rights organizations will, I hope, soon book passage to Cuba to stand with Cuban civil rights activists trying to get some of their members out of the Castros' prisons where they are held in cells with common criminals." [vi]

"Here in this dark box where they make me live, I will be resisting until freedom for my people is gained,' declared Dr. Oscar Elias Biscet, in the vain hope any of the 'news' agencies bestowed 'press' bureaus by his torturer would report the plight of Cuba's political prisoners." [vii]

When you embrace the enemies of your government while at the same time ignoring true freedom fighters, you cannot go wrong. Unfortunately, some of our people did not get the 411 to keep their mouths shut about Cuban racism, as seen here:

"A group of 60 African American artists and thinkers launched a rare — and some say unprecedented — attack on Cuba's human rights record, with a particular focus on the treatment of black political dissidents.

"In a statement issued in November, luminaries including Princeton professor Cornel West, actress Ruby Dee and director Melvin Van Peebles criticized the communist government for its '"increased violations of civil and human rights for those black activists in Cuba who dare raise their voices against the island's racial system."' [viii]

One of the signatories to that statement is Rev. Jeremiah Wright who traveled to Cuba in 1984 with Rev. Jesse Jackson.

Speaking of Cuban racism, it behooves you to obfuscate the following facts so that your black American constituency does not catch on:

"Now to poor, and especially, to black Cubans, [pre-Castro-era President Fulgencio] Batista was a hero and benefactor, because he was black himself and had always been a champion of social legislation...Cubans roared with mirth over the movie Havana, *staring Castro fan Robert Redford, and produced by Castro fan Sydney Pollock. Reviewers hailed it as 'historically accurate.' One scene shows Batista in a meeting with American gangsters. Batista has blonde hair and blue eyes just like Redford.... Hey, he was a Yankee capitalist lackey, right? So he must have looked like a Yankee capitalist.*

"'Batista was black?!' *gasped a badly freaked Pollock at a Hollywood party* *shortly after the movie came out. He'd run into Andy Garcia who informed* *him, between guffaws.*

"*In fact, a high proportion of Batista's army was black and mulatto, espe-* *cially the officer corps. Castro and Che (Guevarra) murdered 600 of them* *without trial in the first three months of 1959. Even the New York Times* *admits it. Had these massacres taken place anyplace else, they'd be called* *lynchings and the United Nations, NAACP, etc., would raise holy hell.* *Imagine, in any other setting, a lily white regime (like Castro's) lynching sev-* *eral hundred blacks, dumping them in mass graves, then getting a standing* *ovation by the Congressional Black Caucus, Jesse Jackson, Maxine Waters,* *Charlie Rangel and Hollywood! Tom, compared to what Cuban-Americans* *see in the news every day, what Alice found on the other side of the looking* *glass seems perfectly logical.*" [ix]

The Cuban President Batista was Black, Young Jeezy!

Fidel Castro doesn't care about black people, Kanye West.

***

Arab racism in the Motherland of Africa is not to be Mentioned

Arab racism can be a distraction from our main goal of hustling the white man:

"*In Egypt, Tunisia, Morocco, Algeria, Libya, Sudan, Somalia, Eritrea, Maur-* *itania and the rest of the Arab world, Africans are treated as the **** of the* *earth. They are second-class citizens at the very best in their own countries.*

Blacks in these countries cannot aspire to positions of respect or authority. There are hardly Africans in high government positions in Arab governed African countries. Like Brazil, which is just as racially cruel against their black natives, there is no legislation favouring slavery (except in Mauritania). It is simply a way of life that's all. Blacks do not really exist or at best are not humans... If one were to ask Gadhafi why Africans are not high up in his government, he might balk that all Libyans are Africans. In that case, one should go and find out the truth for oneself in the poor sections of town. One would be shocked by the plight of our African kith and kin that constitute the bulk of the population in oil rich Libya and other Northern African countries similarly afflicted with Arab racism. While pretending to champion pan-African interest, he is busy getting rid of black immigrants from Libya... Gadhafi's unbridled urge in modern times to enlarge Arabia inside Africa, is a continuation of the Arab war against Africans and the Arabization of African lands that started in the 7th century CE. Arabs have since settled on one-third of Africa, pushing continuously southwards towards the Atlantic Ocean. Arabs' racial war against black Africa started with their occupation and colonization of Egypt between 637 and 642 CE, decimating the Coptic or black population." [x]

CHAPTER 12

Whatever you do, don't educate black people

"What about black youngsters who hit the books and study after school instead of hitting the streets? Sometimes they are ridiculed as being incog-negro or acting white and the ridicule is often accompanied with life-threatening physical violence. Many blacks, particularly black males, have arrived at the devastating conclusion that academic excellence is a betrayal of their black identity."
— Walter E. Willams

All this talk of 'raising educational standards for black kids' is genocidal. High standards are something white folks invented, which is why you should never encourage excellence in education. You do not need educated black people. Smart black people might expose you for what you are.

It is your *raison d'être* to convince your constituency that academic excellence is for white folks only and has no place in the black community. Encourage average or below average achievement as being faithful to black identity.

The more black children you get to tease others for being studious and therefore trying to be "white," should be considered a milestone towards your success.

It is embarrassing for me to admit, but years ago blacks had more respect for education. As you might imagine, there were very few race pimps, who made their money by fomenting hate in the black community. Lucky for you, Liberals have become "progressive," when it comes to their treatment of blacks, which is why race-pimping opportunities abound...with proper training, of course.

Pop Quiz: Ignorance must be elevated as a virtue as part of being "Authentically Black" because

a. You cannot afford black people becoming knowledgeable

b. You can lose your position in the black community

c. You can lose your cash flow

d. All of the above [1]

Ignore and reject claims that black African and black Caribbean children do well in school and excel academically.

Hint: They're not black enough.

Repeat to your constituency VOUCHERS = RACISM, VOUCHERS = RACISM, VOUCHERS = RACISM. The poor have no right to choices in educational opportunities for their children.

Resist any attempts to make schools accountable for their spending, and God-forbid don't mention "outcomes."

If there is any deviation from this plan, black folks may find out you have been lying to them, playing a con game on them, and taking them for a ride. If this happens, you could find yourself on the business end of an illegal firearm.

For all practical purposes, your black constituency is not your friend. In fact, to a degree black Democrats are your enemy, they just don't know it. You would be wise to treat them as consumers. You are the manufacturer of ignorance, and you always need inventory.

For you, blacks are nothing more than stepping stones and paychecks. You have no right to care about their welfare. You are to care only about yourself.

I repeat from earlier in the publication, you of the Black Politburo must enforce black collective thinking. Individual and independent thinking cannot be tolerated as it will threaten your position; such thinking is not tolerated in communist countries and fascist dictatorships. You, the "Black Taliban," must keep your constituency in fear of not being "black enough." (See Chapter 2).

In order to maintain control, you must tell black people what to think.

"What the hell good is Brown v. Board of Education *if nobody wants it?"* – Bill Cosby

Knowledge of the Constitution is for white folks. Black people have no need to know what their rights are and exactly how the U.S government works. Tell them the Constitution is just a piece of paper written by white racists, and it should be ignored.

The Black Panthers of the 1960's made the mistake of studying the constitution and discovering they had rights just like everyone else. They should have ignored the constitution like good black folks do today.

Aside: Concerning the organization that calls itself the New Black Panther Party — "There Is No New Black Panther Party: An Open Letter from the Dr. Huey P. Newton Foundation" [i]

Huey Newton would lose his blackness today, if they knew he studied the Constitution. Though the original Black Panthers dealt with real Democrat oppression, the NEW Black Panther Party is just the black KKK.

Pop quiz: When Democrats promise more money for black colleges and universities, they are being supportive of black education. But when Republicans promise more money for black colleges and universities... [2]

a. Republicans are showcasing the Republicans' long history of educating blacks

b. Republicans are interested in seeing blacks obtain better educations, ergo better opportunities

c. Republicans just want to keep blacks out of their white colleges.

***

Study Ebonics

Any criticism of Ebonics is quite simply to be referred to as "genocide." Ebonics is a legitimate second language. Repeat that with me: Ebonics is a legitimate second language, just like Spanish, French, Tagalong, Vietnamese, Chinese, Polish, German, or Russian.

Mary Texeira, a California State University at San Bernadino sociology professor said: "Ebonics is a different language; it's not slang as many believe. For many of these students Ebonics is their language, and it should be considered a foreign language. These students should be taught like other students who speak a foreign language." *It's nice that Liberals own Wackademia, now isn't it!*

Ebonics should be given equal footing in the world with other languages. So what that there are no works of literature translated into Ebonics. That's just the white man keeping the language of black folks down. Consider how Ebonics could have revolutionized The Bible:

Psalm 23: *"The Lord is my homeboy. I shall not jive. Though I walk through the shadow of the projects, I will fear no gangbanger."*

What about works of literature?

Romeo and Juliet (Balcony Scene): Romeo, Romeo, wherefore art thou Romeo?

Ebonics translation: *"Yo Ro...Ro! Where you at, Dawg?"*

Julius Caesar: "Friends, Romans, Countrymen, lend me your ears."

Ebonics translation: Julius Caesar: *"Homies, peep this here."*

Why should black children bother learning proper English grammar as learning proper English is for white folks only? Substandard English should always be encouraged in black families. This is how you control your black people.

Fun Fact: When the vocabulary of blacks was limited, white slave owners found them easy to control. Learn from the "masters."

Tell your black constituency that having limited communication skills is being "Authentically Black." Webster's Dictionary should be banned from every home, school, library and church.

"Call this the Ebonicization of education,' This mirrors the philosophy of a Los Angeles English teacher who wrote 'Man vs. Ho' on his classroom's white board, (Wait! Whatever happened to BLACKBOARDS? It must be GENO-CIDE! – Authors) to get his students to learn by discussing the lyrics of the late rapper Tupac Shakur:

'Blaze up, getting' with hos through my pager...'Isn't it condescending to think that poor, black, inner-city students 'need' to be taught in rap before they can master standard English." [ii]

Teach that Ebonics is 'black English.'

David H. Fischer, in his book *Albion Seed*, calls Ebonics a bastardization of Standard English from Britain. British immigrants to Virginia brought over a pre-Revolutionary War dialect that later spread throughout the South. Where Northerners would say, 'I am,' 'you are, 'she isn't' and 'I haven't,' Virginians said 'I be,' 'you be,' 'she ain't,' and 'I hain't.' Southerners tended to embellish vowels and soften consonants, thus 'pretty' became 'puriddy' and 'with' became 'wid.' [iii]

According to Fischer, these speech patterns were regional dialects spoken throughout the south and west of England during the seventeenth century, although, under pressure by fellow Englishmen to speak 'proper English,' these speech patterns began to disappear in England. 'In the twentieth century, says Fischer, 'words like "dis" or "dat" were rarely heard in any part of rural England, but they persisted among poor whites and blacks in the American South.' Over the years a few African-origin words fell in, but, says Fischer, 'The major features of the Virginia accent...were established before African slaves could possibly had much impact on language. [iv]

So what Ebonics is really "White Britonics, "Redneckonics," "Honkonics" or "Crackonics." We just added some chocolate to the white batter, and thus a new language was born.

Who cares that nobody but the ignorant use it. Academic excellence was created to hold black folks down.

Academic excellence is not Authentically Black. Never encourage it.

[1] d. Ignorance must be exalted above knowledge.

[2] If you answered "c" then you are obviously paying attention, and well on your way to fun and prosperity keeping the brothers down.

CHAPTER 13

Monitor Reports of Discrimination Constantly

As the teachings of Booker T. Washington reminds us, you must be part of the class of blacks who make a business of keeping the troubles, the wrongs and the hardships of African Americans before the public. You must, having learned that you are able to make a living out of the troubles of blacks, grow into the settled habit of advertising their wrongs, partly because you want sympathy and partly because it pays. You do not want to lose your grievances, because you do not want to lose your job. You must be of the certain class of race problem-solvers who don't want the patient to get well, because as long as the disease holds out, you have not only an easy means of making a living, but also an easy medium through which to make yourself prominent before the public. [i]

The money is in the disease, not the cure. This is why nobody wants to find a cure for disease, they just want continual treatment. If there is a report of the slightest bit of racism in management or ownership in a white company or institution that does not benefit you personally, proceed to protest, picket, and embarrass the company until they give in to your demands that include contributing to your organization and hiring your friends. Make these white folks feel guilty. If they do not give in to your demands because they know you are just hustling them, declare them an "official white supremacist institution." And if your feelings get hurt, you should know what to do by now?

Hint: "Cry "____ism!"

While you are at it, be on the lookout for cases of racism, be they true or false.

When you find such racism, draft a fundraising letter. In the letter, specify that such cases of racism show why you are needed.

Get the black folks angry and then ask for a check. (If the National Alliance, the KKK, the American Nazis, Aryan Nation, etc. go out of business, you are out of a job. Pray that racism is kept alive.)

Here is a suggested template of an all-purpose fundraising letter:

(Date)

(Your Name)

(Your Address)

(Your City, State, Zip)

Dear Brothers and Sisters of (fill your community):

Recently, (fill in some racially-charged event) *happened. This only proves that racism still exists and will always exist in the United States of Amerikkka.*

Ever since we have been brought here in 1619, we have suffered (example of racism), (example of racism), *and* (example of racism). *And in* (current year) *we still suffer.*

And (another example of racism designed to make blacks angry), (another example of racism designed to make blacks angry), *and* (another example of racism designed to make blacks angry).

This not ought to be. How can we allow such things to happen?

(Your organization) *is on the front lines fighting such racism. We work for you.*

We are fighting an uphill battle. But we cannot fight without your support.

Won't you send $10, $25, $50, $100, $500, $1000, $10,000, $50,000, or any amount to keep us fighting these white racists for you? Use the coupon below. (We accept cash, check (which better not bounce), MasterCard, Visa, Discover, and American Express.)

The faster you send in your donation, the faster we can end racism in this country.

We shall overcome.

Sincerely,

(Your Name and Title)

And be sure to send the letter to wealthy whites who suffer from white guilt. These lists are available at all ACORN offices or just request the list from the Democratic National Committee.

If for some reason there is a dry spell of racial incidents, you may have to create your own to let white people know you are alive. These black students showed just how it is done:

"Last October[1999], several people slipped into the Center for Black Culture and Learning on the campus of Miami University in Oxford, Ohio. They left

photocopies of a crude drawing of a black being hanged, and installed com-
puter screen savers with anti-black messages. There was the usual hulla-
baloo, with black demonstrators stopping traffic, public agonizing about
'racism,' and the university president James Garland promising to recruit
more non-white teachers and students. Blacks wallowed in self-pity, with one
telling reporters, 'It's been a very rough four years here. Every day, you are
reminded of the color of your skin. It's horrible.' Now police have fingerprint
evidence that Nathaniel Snow, president of the Black Student Action Associ-
ation, and his black sidekick Brad Allen were the perpetrators. They were, of
course, in the thick of the March 1999 demonstrations- so much so that Mr.
Allen was arrested for disorderly conduct- and Mr. Snow had an hour-long
meeting with president Garland.

"*Was the university delighted to discover that it is not a cauldron of racism*
after all? Somehow, it was not. According to the Cincinnati Enquirer, *'The*
arrests of the two men shocked and disappointed school officials and stu-
dents.' President Garland now says, 'It's important to realize this was an
isolated incident and we should not generalize from it' -quite the reverse of
his earlier view. One black academic advisor, in what was no doubt also a
complete turnaround, cautioned students not to have 'kneejerk' reactions.
Apparently he needn't worry. The white student reaction the Enquirer
printed as representative was that of a junior who asked, "Why would any-
body want to do something like this...?"[ii]

Another reference example happened when:

"*An interracial couple living in Georgia, Freeman Berry and Sandra Benson*
have been arrested for insurance fraud in connection with a self-adminis-
tered hate crime. In August, their home burned to the ground and the couple
complained of hate calls and spray-painted swastikas. There was wide, sym-
pathetic coverage. Miss Benson wept in the backyard of her burned-out
house, telling reporters and investigators she was being punished for loving a
black man. The FBI came to solve the hate crime and discovered that the
couple had burned down their own house. Expensive computer equipment

they claimed had been destroyed in the fire was later found in a rented storage locker. Nationwide Insurance rejected their $301,000 damage claim."
iii

Just to make sure that you understand how to create news properly, we offer this final example:

*"In November[1999], the state legislature in Albany, New York, went into a frenzy when anti-black notes were discovered in front of the doors of the offices of two black legislators. 'Kill all niggers because they don't belong here, 'the notes said, and were signed 'Yours truly KKK. 'Darryl Gray, a 35-year-old black janitor has now confessed to typing and distributing the notes. Police are reportedly unable to think of a motive. Mr. Gray has been charged with aggravated harassment and could be sentenced to up to two years in prison."*iv

This should go without saying, since we have mentioned this point many times at this point. However to be clear: You are to only to raise hell when whites commit hate crimes against blacks.

Black commentator Earl Ofari Hutchinson writes:

"In the Pittsburgh suburb of Wilkinsburg, Joseph Kroll, a middle-aged maintenance man, was busily going about his repair duties in the apartment building where he worked. Joseph Healey, an elderly former Catholic priest, was enjoying a bite to eat at a nearby Burger King restaurant. Emil Sanitelevici, a physics student at the University of Pittsburgh, and two other men were eating at a nearby McDonald's restaurant.

"Then, in a moment of rage, Ronald Taylor gunned down Healey, Kroll and Sanitelevici and seriously wounded the other two men. These heinous killings almost certainly were racially motivated: Taylor is black; the three men killed and the two men wounded were white.

"But unlike after other hate crimes, no black leader or organization immediately rushed forth to vigorously denounce the shootings. There was no expression of outrage from black communities, and there was no demand that Taylor be harshly prosecuted under the federal civil rights hate crimes act if he shot the men because they were white. Worse, some blacks quietly shrugged off the killings with the bitter remark that whites have been killing blacks for years and getting away with it, and that there has been no massive explosion of white outrage at the lax treatment of white killers.

"The deafening silence by blacks on this apparent racial outrage against whites instantly drew shouts from some whites that blacks are hypocrites and have a double standard when victims are whites. They're not totally wrong. Black leaders and organizations should have quickly condemned the shootings. The victims of Taylor's rampage were innocents who happened to be in the wrong place at the wrong time and were shot because they were white." v

Remember, "social justice" is nothing more than political theater to you. If you encourage your black constituency to believe that black-on-black crime is no tragedy as opposed to white-on-black crime, it should not be a stretch for them to believe that black-on-white crime is less than no tragedy.

We are not interested in justice for others outside our own community. When we say "Justice for All," we mean "Just Us."

Hutchinson also wrote: *"Their failure to denounce violence against whites, like the suburban Pittsburgh killings, cedes the moral high ground to white supremacists."*

As a soon-to-be black leader, you must be an expert in double standards and hypocrisy.

CHAPTER 14

A Sarcastic look at Victimology

Let's follow the logic of Al Sharpton in demonstrating victomology, an amazing race-pimping strategist.

If you follow the logic of Al Sharpton, black people live in crime-free neighborhoods.

I know that news is shocking, given the statistics that prove otherwise. We are told that black communities have the highest crime rates, when in fact these stats are simply tainted to make black people look bad.

There is no crime in black neighborhoods; there are just white cops who routinely visit black communities to target black people. One tactic these white cops use is called "Stop and Frisk."

The definition of Stop and Frisk is:

The situation in which a police officer who is suspicious of an individual detains the person and runs his hands lightly over the suspect's outer garments to determine if the person is carrying a concealed weapon.

Stop and Frisk is applied indiscriminately, at almost 100 percent in black neighborhoods on black people. In other words, stop and frisk is not applied to non-blacks.

During Stop and Frisk, we all know what happens.

White cops plant drugs or guns on black people, because black people rarely use drugs, and we don't carry guns. Because of these illegally planted guns and drugs, Stop and Frisk and the oppression of white cops accounts for the disproportionate incarceration rates of blacks in the criminal justice system.

Why white cops?

There are no black cops in America. All the cops in America are not only white, but also white racists, in fact. Because *black* cops would not arrest *black* people — at least not real black cops.

I've watched *Law and Order* and other cop shows, and I have seen Hollywood cops, like rapper-turned-cop Ice-T. But he's an actor. In the real world, there can't be black cops, or else they would have to be part of the system that is keeping blacks down.

I know that it is customary for the police to put cops of the same ethnicity in their neighborhoods, and this works for other ethnicities. According to law enforcement psychologists, sometimes people want to talk to people who look like them and have a common cultural bond. However, this has not happened in the black community.

The people arresting black people—unfairly of course—are white cops.

If for some reason America allowed black cops—and I know there aren't any—there would certainly be no blacks in charge of law enforcement.

Have you ever heard of a black police commissioner, police chief, or sheriff?

God-forbid that a black man be put in charge of the Department of Justice. What kind of country would America be, if blacks were to reach the pinnacle of law enforcement?

There is no black law enforcement leadership, because no self-respecting black in power would allow blacks to be targeted, arrested in record numbers, and then fed to the corrupt whitey-controlled criminal justice system.

And that is why there is no possible way there are black lawyers in America.

There was *one*; but he died. The late great Johnny Cochran. [1]

Oh and there was that "sellout" wannabe black lawyer who prosecuted OJ. The dude who dated the white lawyer with whom he worked. He doesn't count, because he is a Stepin Fetchit black lawyer. The passing of Johnny Cochran took the only black lawyer for black people, which is why blacks in America are facing the problems we experience in the criminal justice system.

Because there are no more black lawyers, black people are convicted at outrageous rates. White lawyers can't possibly understand black people's problem. White lawyers collude with the prosecution to lock black people up.

There is a little known conspiracy to arrest all black people...yes, including Oprah.

How else could so many black people end up in prison in disproportionate numbers?

But even if there were black lawyers, they would have to deal with white judges. America would never let a black lawyer become a judge! What are you...crazy?

I know what you think you see, when you watch Judge Joe Brown, but he's not a real lawyer and he's certainly no judge, is he? He's an actor.

Judge Greg Mathis doesn't count; because he was a criminal before he was a judge. There is no way a black man could come out of the criminal justice system as a perp, and become a judge for real. Don't be stupid…another actor.

Judge Lynn Toler, Judge Mablean Ephriam, Judge Glenda Hatchett… actress, actress, actress. Everybody knows that a black woman could never become a judge in white America.

The idea that a black person could get a law degree, then rise high enough to become a judge is ridiculous. What will they want me to believe next? That a black man could sit on the Supreme Court?

"A handkerchief-head, chicken and biscuit eating Uncle Tom" – Spike Lee on SCOTUS Clarence Thomas.

The facts are clear.

No crime is committed by blacks. There are no black cops, no black lawyers, and no black judges. For these things to happen, we'd have to believe in an America that would not allow a black man to lead the Department of Justice.

And we all know that racist America would never elect a black president.

[1] The Lawd done took him too soon!

CHAPTER 15

A Sarcastic Look at Immigration

Does Al Sharpton see himself as the modern day Sojourner Truth, leading Mexicans to freedom via *el ferrocarril subterráneo* –that's "the underground railroad" for you Americans too lazy to have learned Spanish…our soon-to-be new first language.

As if Sharpton hasn't done enough damage in the black community, he now desires to spread his cancer to Hispanics. Let's review what the pimping of black America by Sharpton, Jackson, and that ilk has gotten the black community.

Per capita, lowest home ownership, business ownership, high school graduation rates, college entrance and graduation rates.

But blacks do lead in a few areas, like number of single parent homes, teenage pregnancy rates, abortion rates, unemployment, and blacks in prison, which coincidentally is not per capita!

I say to the Mexicans, "Bienvenidos…Have I got a plan for you!"

Only in the minds of Liberals is it appropriate for a man who has accomplished nothing of note in the black community be dispatched to provide "help."

Who is he helping? The rancher who was shot by an illegal immigrant? The couple who were beaten and robbed by illegal aliens trespassing on that couple's property? Did I mention they are an American couple?

You would be crazy to think that Sharpton was helping the people who pay for his livelihood—the people he pimps.

Sharpton went to Arizona to help the *criminals*; the banditos who are illegally in America. It's the humanitarian thing to do.

Forget the 1.2M people who wait every year to enter the US legally. How stupid are they.

In typical Liberal fashion Sharpton, in his speech Sharpton hearkened back to the days of civil rights for blacks:

The Arizona Immigration Bill is an affront to the civil rights of all Americans and an attempt to legalize racial profiling…I am calling for a coalition of civil rights organizations to work with those in Arizona to resist and overturn this state law that violates the rights of Americans in that state. [i]

Prior to going to Arizona, Sharpton compared Arizona's law again to Jim Crow laws of the South, apartheid in South Africa, and Nazi Germany. [ii]

Ironically, Sharpton conveniently overlooks the fact that his constant references to the violation of civil rights of blacks, Jim Crow laws, and so on are a reflection of the racist policies of the his Democrat Party.

Then Sharpton showcases his ignorance of Civics, as he dismisses Arizona's right as a state to enforce its laws—laws the Federal government apparently is unwilling to enforce.

State's law doesn't supersede "Pimp Law."

According to Sharpton, asking for proper identification by law enforcement when confronting a person accused of violating a traffic law for example is now considered "racial profiling." Given that America is the "melting pot," aren't we ALL being racially profiled if pulled over for a traffic stop?

There is no logical reason for Sharpton to have made this pilgrimage to Arizona, except to get Sharpton in spotlight. Remember that lesson from earlier in the book?

When you consider that reported unemployment in the black community is at 31%–unreported is theorized to be as high as 50%–allowing millions of illegal immigrants to take jobs from Americans should be sacrilegious.

Until you remember how Sharpton gets paid. I almost got you, right!?

If Sharpton's track record of achievement in the black community is any indication, I suggest the Mexicans call the references on his resume. Everything Sharpton touches turns to ghetto; but then, that's the plan, except in this case replace ghetto with barrio.

As Vietnamese foreign minister Nguyen Thatch believed, when he said decades ago:

"We are not without accomplishment. We have managed to distribute poverty equally."

CHAPTER 16

Desperation of race pimp Jesse Jackson

Don't get desperate, and do what Jesse Jackson has begun doing.

Jesse Jackson attended Hewlett-Packard's annual shareholders meeting to spotlight the lack of minorities in high tech. Jackson claims that technology companies discriminate disproportionately in the hiring of "blacks and browns."

According to Jackson, the comparison of blacks not getting high tech jobs versus blacks USE of high-tech is out of whack, or as Earl "Butch" Graves Jr., president and CEO of Black Enterprise magazine put it, "...companies don't come close to hiring or spending what is commensurate with the demographics of their customers."

Only one in fourteen tech workers is black or Latino both in Silicon Valley and nationally. Blacks and Hispanics make up 13.1 and 16.9 percent of the U.S. population, respectively, according to the most recent census data.

"Technology is supposed to be about inclusion, but sadly, patterns of exclusion remains the order of the day," Jackson wrote in a letter released Monday to Apple Inc., Twitter Inc., Facebook Inc., Hewlett-Packard Co., Google Inc. and others.

Jackson claims that he isn't targeting HP, he's just using the company's annual meeting to highlight the broader issue.

The broader issue is that as recently as 2011, Allstate, in alliance with Jackson's RainbowPUSH organization, recognized HP for its commitment to diversity.

Here's more, "Today, HP is the largest company in the world with both a female CEO and CFO and nearly half of our leadership team and Board of Directors are women and minorities. Additionally, nearly 50 years ago, HP established the first Minority Business Program in the United States."

That comment was from a Latino Executive VP of HP.

You cannot allow yourself to become this desperate. If you sense this coming, be sure to call us on the hotline.

1-555-RACE-BAIT

CHAPTER 17

Let's apply our techniques to Ferguson, Missouri

If there is a perfect example of race-pimping done to perfection, it comes in the aftermath of the shooting of Michael Brown, Jr by police officer Darren Wilson in Ferguson, Missouri.

Brown was confronted by Ferguson police officer Darren Wilson, and Brown was shot six times. The narrative was immediately set that a cop had killed Brown in cold blood, as Brown was trying to surrender.

Leading up to the shooting, we were informed that the cop had told Brown to "get the fuck off the street," and that Brown and the police officer had words, thereafter.

At some point the police officer got out of his care and various reports confirmed there was a scuffle between Brown and the police officer, where Brown may have hit the cop. Reported, one shot was fired from inside the police vehicle, before Brown fled.

The police officer pursued Brown, and we were told that Brown turned, put his hands up to surrender, where he was shot six time by the police officer.

It was said that the police officer didn't know at the time that Brown had committed a crime. So what are the facts of the crime?

In the robbery that was caught on video surveillance, Michael Brown Jr, robbed a convenience store in what is deemed a strong-arm robbery. He stole cigars typically used to roll a type of marijuana cigarette known as a "blunt."

In the video, Brown is seen assaulted the store owner, then sauntering out of the store without a care in the world.

Prior to the video being released, the media immediately Brown as a choir boy, actually referring to him as a "gentle giant...who was on his way to college within days" of the incident.

As for race-pimping, it was necessary to be first in the narrative. Black people are in danger!

To have a hero, we need a demon. So a cop with no record of racial discord in Ferguson must now be made to be a brutal white supremacist who targets black youth.

The looting began, because what God-fearing black community would allow a gentle black teen to be shot and not loot?!

Pavlov had rung the race-baiting bell. *Chapter 13 - Monitor*

Justice Arrives

During the looting, the city of Ferguson became awash in race-pimps. Jesse Jackson and Al Sharpton were smiling like college Liberals men with a fresh supply of Rohypnol, as they descended upon Ferguson.

Without an iota of evidence, Sharpton spoke various times (Chapter 8 – Handling the Media) about justice, and this case, trying to tie it to the handful of cases where the police perhaps wrongly shot cops.

Jackson showed up and actually tried to make the event a fundraiser for his struggling organization.

Pimps in training like Marc Lamont Hill and Van Jones showed up as media, as their reputations were built on events like this. They use these types of events to prove their blackness, standing proudly with protesters in order to profiteer down the road.

But the biggest of the race pimps are in government.

Barack Obama sent in HNIC Eric Holder. When Holder arrived on the scene, he looked like he was filming a modern-day version of *Superfly*, doing a few photo-ops before he would personally pulled the lever that released the scaffold that would lynch Officer Darren Wilson.

A host of local black Liberals called for more diversity in the Ferguson Police Department. This is because diversity equals money for the right people...Leftist who have diversity agenda at the ready.

Just so we are clear, understand that black people who shouted "Kill the cops!" want the Ferguson PD to hire more black cops.

Young black students on the conveyor belt of racism demanded the following:

- A swift and impartial investigation by the Department of Justice into the Mike Brown shooting, and expanded DOJ investigation into civil rights violations across North St. Louis County
- The immediate arrest of Officer Darren Wilson
- County prosecutor Bob McCulloch to stand down and allow special prosecutor to be appointed
- The firing of Ferguson Police Chief Tom Jackson
- Accountability for police practices and policies, including effective civilian review of shootings and allegations of misconduct
- The immediate de-escalation of militarized policing of protestors to protect constitutional rights

- The immediate release of individuals who have been arrested while attending a protest

These youngsters said that if demands are not met, the group would continue to protest. If Officer Wilson is not indicted, the protestors would turn to boycotts and other walk outs.

"We have nothing but time on our hands," said the leader of the group. "We're not going to stop until we get justice, not only for Mike Brown; for everybody, until the whole system understands that we're people, and everyone needs equality."

Despite having nothing to threaten with, this teen understands that media is important, as is making demands you are powerless to accomplish.

As the violence and tension in Ferguson Missouri moved into its second week, we had heard many stories about Michael Brown's guilt and ideas around his innocence. There is no doubt that Brown was a victim. But there was a second victim.

No cop wants to shoot a citizen, unless he is a psychopath. And as information leaked out about the whole story, it became evident that Wilson was attacked, and responded in what had to be an extremely difficult action.

But the media bad guy wasn't supposed to get sympathy.

Forget Wilson's smashed orbital bone, something he received in the apparent beating he took from the 6'4" 300 pound "gentle giant." And what about the mental anguish?

For the Left, there can be only one victim, and this Michael Brown, Jr.

Al Sharpton won't even consider the store owner a victim, as he minimized Brown's theft as "shoplifting." And there are many other apologists who needed to keep Michael Brown as the sole victim.

There were many victims, like the business owners. They put their livelihoods at stake, investing in the black community. Their reward was to have their businesses looted, in many cases as cops who were mandated to "stand down," watching as two dozen or more businesses were looted, some of them more than once; stripped of any merchandise on their shelves and destroyed.

Did the manager of the Quick Trip convenience store pull the trigger? He was not there the day that Michael Brown lost his life, yet he was made to pay the price.

Several business owners stood in front of their stores with their own personal legally-owned weapons. Whether or not those businesses will rebuild in Ferguson is uncertain. Yet there will soon be calls for more jobs for black people, and more businesses in black neighborhoods, by the race pimps.

They will demand jobs for an economically depressed area, while making sure that the places that might have offered those very jobs take the hit for "justice." Force businesses to move into the war zones, because that strategy always works.

And what about the neighborhood residents, who are victims as well. For almost two weeks, Ferguson resident were forced to endure countless champions of truth and civil rights cut across their front and back yards, leaving trash and debris behind in their neighborhoods. In a time of unseasonably good weather, the Ferguson residents didn't enjoy it, since tear gas tends to impact fresh air, as do the constant wail of sirens and the rumble of bullhorns telling crowds to move.

This is a time that any child over the age of five in Ferguson will remember for the rest of his life. One of the reasons they will remember this is because they were unable to start school on time this year.

The Ferguson-Florissant School District (of which the city of Ferguson is a part) delayed the start of the school year until August 25. School was supposed to start approximately two weeks prior. Some of the most militant may argue that Ferguson's children are getting an education that they would not be taught in school. Would that militant education include how to make flaming bottles of gasoline and resisting the police? The education of some 12,000 students is now in the hands of people who feel they "deserve" the chance to loot, riot, pillage and destroy the property and livelihoods of hard working citizens because, they demand justice.

But don't expect any sympathy from those who wish to make this a cops versus blacks meme. For them, there is only one victim. The gentle giant known as Michael Brown.

Epilogue

Well, that's it.

You are well on your way to becoming a black race pimp and a profitable one at that!

This book is a working manual, your bible, so don't be afraid to write in it, and you should keep it with you at all times.

We have included work from the "Dark Side" in this area, along with the earlier areas where we warned you. You need to know your competition, or in this case those who could put you out of business. Use this information to understand the other side, so that you can see potential roadblocks.

Here's to champagne tastes and caviar dreams!

Nannie Helen Burroughs was an educator, orator, religious leader, and businesswoman. She gained national recognition for her 1900 speech "How the Sisters Are Hindered from Helping," at the National Baptist Convention.

Burroughs was born on May 2, 1879, in Orange, Virginia to John and Jennie Burroughs, who were both ex-slaves. Her father was a farmer and itinerant Baptist preacher, her mother a cook.

After the death of her father when Burroughs was five, she and her younger sister were brought to Washington, D.C. by their mother in pursuit of a better education.

In 1896, Burroughs graduated with honors in business and domestic science from the Colored High School on M Street (now Dunbar High School).

She received an honorary M.A. degree from Eckstein-Norton University in Kentucky in 1907.

In 1896, Burroughs helped establish the National Association of Colored Women (NACW). In 1897, Burroughs started work as an associate editor at the Christian Banner in Philadelphia, Pa.

In 1900, Burroughs moved to Louisville, Kentucky, to work as a secretary for the Foreign Mission Board of the National Baptist Convention.

In 1909, she founded the National Training School for Women and Girls in Washington, D.C., which was renamed in her honor the Nannie Helen Burroughs School after her death and is a National Historic Landmark.

The school emphasized preparing students for real employment. As such, Burroughs offered courses in domestic science and secretarial skills, as well as more unconventional occupations such as shoe repair, barbering, and gardening.

Burroughs created a creed of racial self-help through her program of the three Bs: the Bible, the bath, and the broom. The Bible, the bath, and the broom stood for a clean life, a clean body, and a clean house.

She believed domestic work should be professionalized and even unionized. Burroughs trained her students to become respectable employees by becoming pious, pure, and domestic, but not submissive. She emphasized the importance of being proud black women to all students, by teaching black history and culture through a required course in the Department of Negro History.

Burroughs died in Washington D.C. on May 20, 1961. A street in the Deanwood neighborhood of the city is named after her, specifically Nannie Helen Burroughs Avenue NE.

Even in a time of Jim Crow and legal segregation, Nannie Helen Burroughs did not wallow in pity and self-despair as any normal black victim of today would, and this is why you need to know about her.

Be able to counter her evil, empowering ways.

12 Things The Negro Must Do For Himself by Nannie Helen Burroughs

1. The Negro Must Learn To Put First Things First. The First Things Are: Education; Development of Character Traits; A Trade and Home Ownership.

The Negro puts too much of his earning in clothes, in food, in show and in having what he calls "a good time." The Dr. Kelly Miller said, "The Negro buys what he WANTS and begs for what he needs." Too true!

2. The Negro Must Stop Expecting God and White Folk To Do For Him What He Can Do For Himself.

It is the "Divine Plan" that the strong shall help the weak, but even God does not do for man what man can do for himself. The Negro will have to do exactly what Jesus told the man (in John 5:8) to do—Carry his own load —"Take up your bed and walk."

3. The Negro Must Keep Himself, His Children And His Home Clean And Make The Surroundings In Which He Lives Comfortable and Attractive.

He must learn to "run his community up"—not down. We can segregate by law, we integrate only by living. Civilization is not a matter of race; it is a matter of standards. Believe it or not—some day, some race is going to outdo the Anglo-Saxon, completely. It can be the Negro race, if the Negro gets sense enough. Civilization goes up and down that way.

4. The Negro Must Learn To Dress More Appropriately For Work And For Leisure.

Knowing what to wear—how to wear it—when to wear it and where to wear it are earmarks of common sense, culture and also an index to character.

5. The Negro Must Make His Religion An Everyday Practice And Not Just A Sunday-Go-To-Meeting Emotional Affair.

6. The Negro Must Highly Resolve To Wipe Out Mass Ignorance.

The leaders of the race must teach and inspire the masses to become eager and determined to improve mentally, morally and spiritually, and to meet the basic requirements of good citizenship.

We should initiate an intensive literacy campaign in America, as well as in Africa. Ignorance—*satisfied ignorance*—is a millstone about the neck of the race. It is democracy's greatest burden.

Social integration is a relationship attained as a result of the cultivation of kindred social ideals, interests and standards.

It is a blending process that requires time, understanding and kindred purposes to achieve. Likes alone and not laws can do it.

7. The Negro Must Stop Charging His Failures Up To His "Color" And To White People's Attitude.

The truth of the matter is that good service and conduct will make senseless race prejudice fade like mist before the rising sun.

God never intended that a man's color shall be anything other than a *badge of distinction*. It is high time that all races were learning that fact. The Negro must first QUALIFY for whatever position he wants. Purpose, initiative, ingenuity and industry are the keys that all men use to get what they want. The Negro will have to do the same. He must make himself a workman who is too skilled not to be wanted, and too DEPENDABLE not to be on the job, according to promise or plan. He will never become a vital factor in industry until he learns to put into his work the vitalizing force of initiative, skill and dependability. He has gone "RIGHTS" mad and "DUTY" dumb.

8. The Negro Must Overcome His Bad Job Habits.

He must make a brand new reputation for himself in the world of labor. His bad job habits are absenteeism, funerals to attend, or a little business to look after. The Negro runs an off and on business. He also has a bad reputation for conduct on the job—such as petty quarrelling with other help, incessant loud talking about nothing; loafing, carelessness, due to lack of job pride; insolence, gum chewing and—too often—liquor drinking. Just plain bad job habits!

9. He Must Improve His Conduct In Public Places.

Taken as a whole, he is entirely too loud and too ill-mannered.

There is much talk about wiping out racial segregation and also much talk about achieving integration.

Segregation is a physical arrangement by which people are separated in various services.

It is definitely up to the Negro to wipe out the apparent justification or excuse for segregation.

The only effective way to do it is to clean up and keep clean. By practice, cleanliness will become a habit and habit becomes character.

10. The Negro Must Learn How To Operate Business For People—Not For Negro People, Only.

To do business, he will have to remove all typical "earmarks," business principles; measure up to accepted standards and meet stimulating competition, graciously—in fact, he must learn to welcome competition.

11. The Average So-Called Educated Negro Will Have To Come Down Out Of The Air. He Is Too Inflated Over Nothing. He Needs An Experience Similar To The One That Ezekiel Had—(Ezekiel 3:14-19). And He Must Do What Ezekiel Did

Otherwise, through indifference, as to the plight of the masses, the Negro, who thinks that he has escaped, will lose his own soul. It will do all leaders good to read Hebrew 13:3, and the first thirty-seven chapters of Ezekiel.

A race transformation itself through its own leaders and its sensible "common people." A race rises on its own wings, or is held down by its own weight. True leaders are never "things apart from the people." They are the masses. They simply got to the front ahead of them. Their only business at the front is to inspire to masses by hard work and noble example and challenge them to "Come on!" Dante stated a fact when he said, "Show the people the light and they will find the way!"

There must arise within the Negro race a leadership that is not out hunting bargains for itself. A noble example is found in the men and women of the Negro race, who, in the early days, laid down their lives for the people. Their invaluable contributions have not been appraised by the "latter-day leaders." In many cases, their names would never be recorded, among the unsung heroes of the world, but for the fact that white friends have written them there.

"Lord, God of Hosts, Be with us yet."

The Negro of today does not realize that, but, for these exhibits A's, that certainly show the innate possibilities of members of their own race, white people would not have been moved to make such princely investments in lives and money, as they have made, for the establishment of schools and for the on-going of the race.

12. The Negro Must Stop Forgetting His Friends. "Remember."

Read Deuteronomy 24:18. Deuteronomy rings the big bell of gratitude. Why? Because an ingrate is an abomination in the sight of God. God is constantly telling us that *"I the Lord thy God delivered you"*— through human instrumentalities.

The American Negro has had and still has friends—in the North and in the South. These friends not only pray, speak, write, influence others, but make unbelievable, unpublished sacrifices and contributions for the advancement of the race—for their brothers in bonds.

The noblest thing that the Negro can do is to so live and labor that these benefactors will not have given in vain. The Negro must make his heart warm with gratitude, his lips sweet with thanks and his heart and mind resolute with purpose to justify the sacrifices and stand on his feet and go forward—*"God is no respector of persons. In every nation, he that feareth him and worketh righteousness is"* sure to win out. Get to work! That's the answer to everything that hurts us. We talk too much about nothing instead of redeeming the time by working.

R-E-M-E-M-B-E-R

In spite of race prejudice, America is brim full of opportunities. Go after them!

The Poverty Pimp's Poem

Let us celebrate the poor,

Let us hawk them door to door.

There's a market for their pain,

Votes and glory and money to gain.

Let us celebrate the poor.

Their ills, their sins, their faulty diction

Flavor our songs and spice our fiction.

Their hopes and struggles and agonies

Get us grants and consulting fees.

Celebrate thugs and clowns,

Give their ignorance all renown.

Celebrate what holds them down,

In our academic gowns.

Let us celebrate the poor. [i]

How to Run an Effective Boycott

"1. Research all possible targets. Choose a target that is likely to yield to your demands and that will gain the support of consumers.

"2. Get all the facts about the company and the offensive policy or action. It may be more difficult to get information from the company later. Use the company's annual reports (readily available at the library or posted on the Internet) to obtain important company information such as product and brand names, the president and/or CEO's name(s), and addresses and phone numbers. Be ready to justify why you chose your target to consumers and the media.

"3. Write to or meet with the company to voice your grievance. Indicate that if the policy or action is not changed, you intend to initiate a consumer boycott.

"4. Occasionally the threat of a boycott can make the company yield to your demands. Some organizers attempt to negotiate with the company first and use a boycott strategy only if negotiations fail to bring about the desired changes.

"5. Organize a coalition that includes the support or endorsements of other organizations. Be prepared to present numbers to the company to show the support for and strength of the boycott." [ii]

Threaten lawsuits. Black writer Elizabeth Wright reports:

"In the Winter 1997 edition of Issues & Views, writer Shahrazad Ali described the antics of blacks who either had filed class-action lawsuits or were plotting lawsuits against their white employers for so-called discriminatory practices. Calling this stratagem 'a new job related lottery,' she chided such blacks for their 'perpetual begging' and willingness to have whites 'buy and sell' them. Thanks to today's political climate, the perpetual begging has turned into perpetual demands—with more than a hint of punishment for any corporate executive who's too dense to understand the nature of the times we live in.

"Although several previous lawsuits had set precedents for their large bounties, the victory in 1996 over Texaco, Inc. set a new standard for bounty hunters. More so, this case confirmed for new generations of blacks that protest and confrontation are still effective means to redistribute the wealth. The 1960s route to fame and comfort is now ingrained as a method and seems certain to remain a fixture in black culture. The lesson is absorbed early by the young. They soon deduce that, while members of other groups are expected to employ conventional paths to affluence, blacks have a special formula reserved for them. And, daily, black leaders confirm that it's a formula that works... And so the formula is fixed: First seek out a provable rash remark made by some bonehead white official who still doesn't know what time of day it is. Then broadcast his blunder far and wide, while your 'leaders' loudly rail in indignation about racism and white arrogance and threaten boycotts and lawsuits. Next, while the flabbergasted corporate *moguls flail around and futilely defend themselves, move in the troops and show them who really is in charge. From there on, it's a gravy train."* [iii]

Threaten anything:

"[Michael] *McGee knew how to provoke a reaction, put you on edge, and keep you there. I have always respected that ability in a person. Even if the line of thinking isn't always rational, even if the personality grates, it forces you to respond. McGee was heavily invested in pushing buttons. When Jimmy Carter came to Milwaukee to build houses for Habitat for Humanity, McGee and some of his entourage showed up and began blowing whistles and carrying signs that read 'Missionaries Out of Milwaukee' and 'Jobs, Not Charity'—all for the benefit of Good Morning America. When the Common Council posed for its official 1988 portrait, McGee wore a paper bag over his head—his own Ku Klux Klan-type protest over the company he was forced (by election) to keep. On two occasions, once in 1987 and again in 1990, he threatened to disrupt an event that is near and dear to the heart of most Milwaukeeans—the Great Circus Parade. In the first instance he was going to throw eggs; in the second, he was going to try to shut it down altogether, a threat that was answered with a legal injunction."* [iv]

Am I Black Enuf for Ya?

by Keith Wilson

If I told you that I couldn't rap or sing, that I couldn't dance to save my life, and that I don't even shoot hoops that well, would you say that I'm not black enuf for ya?

If you saw that I don't wear big gold chains, that I don't have dreadlocks or a huge Jackson Five afro, or that I don't have a cool nickname like Ice or Smooth, would I not be black enuf for ya?

If I don't drink Ripple, Cisco, or Hennessey, if I've never sold drugs, and if I've never been arrested, am I not black enuf for ya?

If I allow you to run a credit check on me, and you learn that not only do I have a job, but that I pay my bills on time, would you think that I'm not black enuf for ya?

If I fail to start every sentence with "Yo', Dawg," or if I refuse to refer to my sistas as bitches 'n hoes, am I not black enuf for ya?

If I don't brag about having four kids by four different women, or if I don't eagerly proclaim that the white man is the devil, are you going to wonder if I'm black enuf for ya?

If I don't cheat on my woman and diminish her self-esteem, place in society as the Queen that deserves to be, does this mean I'm not black enuf for ya?

If I secretly admit that I really do like Seinfeld, or that I actually know how to swim, or that I honestly think OJ did do it, would I not be black enuf for ya?

See, I'm not sure, how many of your stereotypes do I have to fulfill before you reinstate my official ghetto pass? Where do I apply for admission to this mythical club of blackness that you seem to think I should belong to?

Be-cuz the truth is - I KNOW who I am.

See, long ago, I responded to this advertisement that ran in the newspaper of my mind:

WANTED — hardworking, intelligent, and articulate individual, must be sensitive, but strong; philosophical, but playful. Candidate must have a pulsating passion for life, an unquenchable thirst for knowledge, and an unlimited supply of determination. Must be able to bear the weight of your history and to carry the hopes of your ancestors. Must also be able to demonstrate an ability to dream while awake, and a willingness to achieve by any means necessary. Qualified candidate must possess own recipe for survival, including the ability to locate a grain of laughter amidst a field of despair. It will be necessary to have rhythm in your soul and soul in your rhythm, along with a willingness to embrace sorrow and reject cowardly hatred. Physical requirements include arms that are long enough to reach back into the community, but are too short to box with God. Prefer skin that is like midnight satin, but am willing to consider creamy cocoa brown, Hershey's dark chocolate, honey-dipped high yellow, sun-kissed redbone, and even light, bright, and almost white. Can fall anywhere between Denzel fine and Dennis Rodman thru, between Coltrane's intensity and Miles Davis cool. Hair-optional; height-irrelevant; big feet a definite plus. (You know what I'm talkin' 'bout.) Priority consideration given to self-respecting, sure stepping, confidence oozing, brown-eyed, thick-lipped, wide-nosed warriors. Timid, shuffling, droop-shouldered, apologetic, self-loathing, self-destructive Uncle Clarence Thomases need not apply. If interested, please inquire within.

So, if I show you my ID card that says "Grade A, Inspected, Certified 100% Sho' Nuff [http://en.wikipedia.org/wiki/Sho%27_Nuff] Brotha," then, I ask you, then, will I be black enuf for ya?

Be sure to get Kevin Jackson's other best-selling books:

The BIG Black Lie…How I learned the truth about the Democratic Party

Sexy Brilliance and Other Political Lies

References

Foreword

[i]   http://www.discriminations.us/2008/02/%E2%80%9Cdiversity%E2%80%9D-money-%E2%80%94-well-spent/

[ii] ibid

[iii] http://www.workforce.com/section/11/feature/23/42/49/index.html

Chapter 1

[i]   http://www.wnd.com/2013/03/suburbs-secede-from-atlanta/#r3S4pv97x4XYSJJ6.99

[ii] "Pseudo Leadership And Black Groupthink," LaShawn Barber, LaShawn-Barber.com, October 5, 2004, http://lashawnbarber.com/archives/2004/10/05/pseudo/

[iii] Ken Hamblin, Pick a Better Country, (New York: Simon & Shuster, 1996), p. 45

iv http://en.wikiquote.org/wiki/Booker_T._Washington

v Tony Brown, *Black Lies, White Lies*, (New York: William Morrow and Co., Inc, 1995), p.46

vi "A Reminder of Why They Still Owe Us," Dr. Conrad Worrill, The Black Commentator,   http://www.blackcommentator.com/265/265_worrills_world_reminder_owe_us.html

vii   http://web.archive.org/web/20100926031018/http:/www.columbiabso.org/?page_id=118

Chapter 2

i http://espn.go.com/sportscentury/features/00016393.html

ii http://baltimorechronicle.com/blackvote_nov02.shtml

iii Debra J. Dickerson, *The End of Blackness*, (New York: Pantheon Books, 2004), p.132

iv   http://www.washingtonpost.com/wp-dyn/content/article/2007/02/15/AR2007021501270.html

v "Obama's Appeal to Blacks Remains an Open Question,"Michael A. Fletcher, January 25, 2007, http://www.washingtonpost.com/wp-dyn/content/article/2007/01/24/AR2007012402032_pf.html

vi "Black American from Africa offers his view on Obama's 'blackness'," Willis Shalita, *San Francisco Chronicle*, March 1, 2007, http://www.sfgate.com/cgi-bin/article.cgi?f=/c/a/2007/03/01/EDGRJN7A981.DTL#ixzz1I2kioOI9

vii The New Black Nativism," *Time*, February 8, 2007, http://www.time.com/time/magazine/article/0,9171,1587276,00.html

viii From "How Authentically Black Are You? A Secret Formula to Help You Out," http://www.thecolorcurve.com/blog/theintel/how-authentically-black-are-you-a-secretformula-to-help-you-out/

ix "Deep Black Sea," *How to be Black*, June 11, 2010, http://how-to-be-black.blogspot.com/2010/06/deep-black-sea.html

x http://www.tampabay.com/opinion/columns/code-of-silence-corrodes-morality-puts-blacks-at-risk/1110709

xi Juan Williams, *Enough: The Phony Leaders, Dead-End Movements, and Culture of Failure That Are Undermining Black America—and What We Can Do About It*, (New York: Crown Publishers, 20060, pp. 111-114.

xii May 20, 2008, http://blacksnob.blogspot.com/2008/05/definition-of-blackness.html

xiii Libs Scold Black Conservatives," Lloyd Marcus, *American Thinker*, December 21, 2009, http://www.americanthinker.com/2009/12/libs_scold_black_conservatives.html

xiv John McWhorter, *Losing the Race* (New York: The Free Press, 2000), pp. 41-42

xv John McWhorter, *Losing the Race*, p. 3

xvi http://articles.latimes.com/1997/aug/09/news/mn-20771

xvii Black leaders back Cosby's straight talk," http://www.washington-times.com/news/2004/jul/4/20040704-121543-2465r/

xviii Ken Hamblin, *Pick a Better Country*, (New York: Simon & Schuster, 1997), pp. 102-103

xix John McWhorter, *Losing the Race*, pp. 29-31

xx Shelby Steele, The Content of Our Character, p.23

xxi Shelby Steele, The Content of Our Character, pp. 23-24

Chapter 3

[i] Tony Brown, *Black Lies, White Lies*, p. 123

[ii] http://www.humanevents.com/article.php?id=16588

[iii] http://www.judicialwatch.org/archive/2006/jackson-report.pdf

[iv] "REV. AL SOAKS UP BOYCOTT BUCKS: BIZ GIANTS PAY OR FACE RACE RALLIES," Isabel Vincent and Susan Edelman, *New York Post*, June 15, 2008, http://www.nypost.com/p/news/regional/item_83CBBYg-MujzxLtqgHzPAuN#ixzz1I1UhaZxh

[v] http://onedetroitnetwork.blogspot.com/2007/04/black-liberals-need-to-stop-double.html

[vi] http://www.blackgenocide.org/negro.html

[vii] Jim Sleeper, *Liberal Racism*, (New York: The Penguin Group, 1997), pp. 23-25

[viii] http://www.telegraph.co.uk/news/worldnews/africaandindianocean/nigeria/10808830/Nigerian-Islamist-leader-threatens-to-sell-abducted-girls-as-slaves.html

[ix] http://www.afrocentricnews.com/html/myth_of_african_unity.html

[x] http://lashawnbarber.com/archives/2007/01/02/selective-outrage-over-black-crime-victims

[xi] http://en.wikipedia.org/wiki/Crime_in_South_Africa

[xii] "Extending Concern To Black-on-black Repression, Too," Clarence Page, *Chicago Tribune*, July 19, 1989, http://articles.chicagotribune.com/1989-07-19/news/8902180623_1_african-american-south-african-leaders-congressional-black-caucus

xiii "This Silence Is Not Golden," *The Field Negro*, April, 6, 2006, http://field-negro.blogspot.com/2006/04/this-silence-is-not-golden.html

xiv http://members.aol.com/casmasalc/sorrow_shame.html)

xv Eric Rush, *Negrophilia*, p. xix

xvi ibid p.17

xvii Tony Brown, *Black Lies, White Lies*, p.57

Chapter 4

i http://www.balloon-juice.com/2011/01/27/the-white-sheets-come-out-of-the-senate-closet/

ii Bruce Bartlett, *Wrong on Race*, (New York: Palgrave Macmillan, 2008), p. 107

iii ibid p. 108

iv http://www.black-and-right.com/the-democrat-race-lie/

v "I am a Lincoln Republican," Yervand Kochar, *American Thinker*, November 14, 2009, http://www.americanthinker.com/2009/11/i_am_a_lincoln_republican_1.html

vi Thomas Sowell, *Black Rednecks and White Liberals*, (New York: Encounter Books, 2005), p. 114

vii Jim Sleeper, *Liberal Racism*, p. 101

viii "Digging Kunta Kinte," Jack White, *The Root*, February 28, 2008, http://www.theroot.com/views/digging-kunta-kinte

ix "Black History Urban Legends," Audrey Peterson, *American Legacy Magazine*, March 6, 2009, http://www.rjrmediagroup.com/wordpress_blog/?tag=black-history-urban-legends

x Shelby Steele, The Content of Our Character, pp. 34-35

Chapter 5

i http://en.wikipedia.org/wiki/Joe_Louis_vs._Max_Schmeling

ii http://www.tv.com/george-foreman/person/32501/trivia.html

iii http://www.urbanfaith.com/2010/11/wheres-the-change.html

iv http://www.youtube.com/watch?v=jSUEbdebWjY

v http://www.mynorthwest.com/?nid=76&sid=129529

vi http://www.youtube.com/watch?v=P36x8rTb3jI

vii Book Review of *Accountable*, BlackNews.com, http://www.black-news.com/news/tavis_smiley_accountable_book_review101.shtml

viii http://www.wnd.com/?pageId=82309

ix "AP Finds Race Hustler to Say Obama Isn't The Cure," http://newsbusters.org/blogs/warner-todd-huston/2008/11/25/ap-finds-race-hustler-say-obama-isnt-cure#ixzz1GhonPZE7

x "My Guy, Wrong or Wrong," Joel Engel, The Death of Common Sense, September 23, 2010, http://thedeathofcommonsense.latimesmagazine.com/2010/09/my-guy-wrong-or-wrong.html

Chapter 6

ⁱ Jim Sleeper, *Liberal Racism*, pp. 18-19

ⁱⁱ http://www.blackgenocide.org

Chapter 7

ⁱ http://www.pressdemocrat.com/article/20100611/ARTICLES/100619856

ⁱⁱ http://www.youtube.com/watch?v=0FIBJt-c2o0

ⁱⁱⁱ "As the Media Start to Enshrine Byrd, Questions About His Legacy Endure," Bob Parks, BigJournalism.com, June 28, 2010, http://bigjourn-alism.com/bparks/2010/06/28/as-the-media-start-to-enshrine-byrd-ques-tions-about-his-legacy-endure/

ⁱᵛ "Dem. Sen. Byrd's True "Racist" Legacy – 'KKK Exalted Cyclops,' Bruce Eden,   nationalwriterssyndicate.com,http://nationalwriterssyndicate.com/index2.php?option=com_content&do_pdf=1&id=2037

ᵛ Joseph Perkins, *Jewish World Review*, February 23, 2001, http://www.jewishworldreview.com/cols/perkins022301.asp

ᵛⁱ http://en.wikipedia.org/wiki/Gulag

ᵛⁱⁱ Shelby Steele, *A Dream Deferred*, (New York: Harper Collins Publishers, 1998), pp. 6-7

ᵛⁱⁱⁱ "The Day I Got The Juan Williams Treatment: A Wake-Up Call To Bloggers Everywhere," The Obsidian, *The Spearhead*, November 4, 2010, http://www.the-spearhead.com/2010/11/04/the-day-i-got-the-juan-wil-liams-treatment-a-wake-up-call-to-bloggers-everywhere/

ⁱˣ Debra J. Dickerson, *The End of Blackness*, pp. 173-174

ˣ Tony Brown, *Black Lies, White Lies*, pp. 71-72

ˣⁱ Debra J. Dickerson, *The End of Blackness*, pp. 177-179

xii "Tavis Smiley Beating White Man's Drum of Nazi Superiority," Creole Folks, Newsvine.com, January 14, 2011, http://creolefolks.newsvine.com/_news/2011/01/14/5841751-tavis-smiley-beating-white-mans-drum-of-nazi-superiority-creole-folks

xiii "Disproportionate Representation of African American Students in Special Education: Acknowledging the Role of White Privilege and Racism," Wanda J. Blanchett, *Educational Researcher*, June 5, 2006, http://www.aera.net/uploadedFiles/Publications/Journals/Educational_Researcher/3506/06ERv35n6_Blanchett.pdf

Chapter 8

i http://www.answers.com/topic/al-sharpton

ii http://www.adl.org/main_Extremism/new_black_panther_party.htm

iii   http://lormarie.com/2010/04/27/white-woman-gets-raped-by-a-black-man-and-its-the-white-mans-fault/

iv "No 'Hate Crime' Charge For Black Teens Arrested For Anti-Asian Murder," therightperspective.org, June 12, 2009, http://www.therightperspective.org/2009/06/12/no-hate-crime-charge-for-black-teens-arrested-for-anti-asian-murder/

v http://www.topix.net/forum/blogs/TEUAG0CA11NPHLQJB

vi "Media Blackout On Christian-Newsom Murders?" LaShawn Barber, LaShawnBarber.com, May 14, 2007, http://lashawnbarber.com/archives/2007/05/14/media-blackout-on-christian-newsom-murders/

vii "Planned Parenthood charged with racism," WorldNetDaily.com, August 19, 2004, http://www.wnd.com/?pageId=26136

Chapter 9

i http://moteandbeam.tripod.com/Uncover_Printout.pdf

ii http://www.oocities.org/ambwww/ezola.htm

Chapter 10

i Juan Williams, *Enough*, p.78

ii http://www.37thtexas.org/html/BlkHist.html

Chapter 11

i "Romancing the Dictators, Jack White, *The Root*, February 28, 2011, http://www.theroot.com/views/romancing-dictators

ii**"Advice to Africa: Keep Your Whites,"** *AIM Report*, July 1997, https://www.campusreportonline.net/publications/aim_report/1997/07a.htm

iii "Fidel Castro at 80: Is He Our Friend or Foe?", William Jelani Cobb, *AOL Black Voices*, August 8, 2006, http://www.blackvoices.com/black_news/canvas_directory_headlines_features/_a/fidel-castro-at-80-is-he-our-friend-or/20060810075609990001

iv "Rush, Jesse, and Fidel," Humberto Fontova, *American Thinker*, October 17, 2009, http://www.americanthinker.com/2009/10/rush_jesse_jackson_and_fidel.html

v "On Jesse Jackson," CapitolHillCubans.com, March 3, 2011, http://www.capitolhillcubans.com/2011/03/on-jesse-jackson.html

vi "The Castro Brothers' Big Dirty Secret," Nat Hentoff, Offnews.info, April 1, 2010, http://www.offnews.info/verArticulo.php?contenidoID=19418

vii "Castro Torture-Victim Nominated for Nobel Peace Prize," Humberto Fontova, February, 24, 2011, http://bigpeace.com/hfontova/2011/02/24/castro-torture-victim-nominated-for-nobel-peace-prize/

viii "Black activists launch rare attack on Cuba about racism," Richard Fausset, *Los Angeles Times*, January 3, 2010,http://articles.latimes.com/2010/jan/03/nation/la-na-cuba-blacks3-2010jan03

ix "The Real Fidel," Thomas E. Woods, Jr., LewRockwell.com, http://www.lewrockwell.com/woods/woods47.html

x**"Arab Racism against Black Africans,"** Naiwu Osahon, http://www.pashtunforums.com/world-news-16/arab-racism-against-black-africans-11072/

Chapter 12

i http://www.blackpanther.org/newsalert.htm

ii*Stupid Black Men*, p. 212

iii ibid

iv*Stupid Black Men*, pp. 212-213

Chapter 13

i *Based on writings of Booker T. Washington, 1911*

ii "State Investigators Enter Miami," Randy McNutt, *Cincinnati Enquirer*, November 14, 1999,"Two Charged in Racial Vandalism," Saundra Amrhein and Kevin Aldridge, *Cincinnati Enquirer*, January 22, 1999, p. A4, Police: Students Faked Slurs, Mark Ferenchik, *The Columbus Dispatch*, January 22, 1999, p. ID

iii "FBI Probes Georgia Insurance Scam," Chelsea Carter, Associated Press, August 24.1997

iv "Black Janitor Accused of Hate Notes," *New York Times*, November. 9, 1999

v "Why Are Black Leaders Silent On Black Hate Crimes?," Earl Ofari Hutchinson, Salon.com, March 6, 2000, http://www.salon.com/news/feature/2000/03/06/hate

Chapter 14

i   http://newsone.com/nation/rev-al-sharpton/sharpton-compares-ariz-immigration-law-to-apartheid-nazi-germany/

ii   http://www.nydailynews.com/ny_local/2010/04/26/2010-04-26_rev_al_plans_immig_rally.html

Epilogue

i http://www.jewishworldreview.com/cols/sowell103098.asp

ii http://www.amerikaos.com/boycottguide.html

iii "Lawsuit Gravy Train: Doing It the Black Way," Elizabeth Wright, GlobalPoltician.com, http://www.globalpolitician.com/print.asp?id=3222

iv Jonathan Coleman, *A Long Way to Go* (Synopsis), http://www.nytimes.com/books/first/c/coleman-longway.html

CPSIA information can be obtained
at www.ICGtesting.com
Printed in the USA
LVOW10s0349060617

537062LV00036B/1701/P

9 781619 339521